Army Forces for Homeland Security

Lynn E. Davis, David E. Mosher, Richard R. Brennan,

Michael D. Greenberg, K. Scott McMahon, Charles W. Yost

Prepared for the United States Army
Approved for public release, distribution unlimited

ARROYO CENTER

The research described in this report was sponsored by the United States
Army under Contract No. DAS01-96-C-003.

Library of Congress Cataloging-in-Publication Data

Army forces for homeland security / Lynn Davis ... [et al.].
    p. cm.
    "MG-221."
    Includes bibliographical references.
    ISBN 0-8330-3673-4 (pbk.)
    1. Civil defense—United States. 2. United States. Army. I. Davis, Lynn E.
(Lynn Etheridge), 1943–.

UA927.A89 2004
363.32'0973—dc22

2004018265

The RAND Corporation is a nonprofit research organization providing
objective analysis and effective solutions that address the challenges
facing the public and private sectors around the world. RAND's
publications do not necessarily reflect the opinions of its research clients
and sponsors.

RAND® is a registered trademark.

*Cover photo, left: U.S. Army Corps of Engineers, New England District, "United States Army
Corps of Engineers New England District Responds to WTC Attack," http://www.nae.usace.
army.mil/wtc/wtc%20photo%20gallery/index.htm (as of June 24, 2004).*

*Cover photo, right: Photo courtesy of New England District of the U.S. Army Corps of
Engineers, at http://www.nae.usace.army.mil. F. T. Eyre, Staff Photographer, U.S. Army Corps
of Engineers.*

© Copyright 2004 RAND Corporation

Published 2004 by the RAND Corporation
1776 Main Street, P.O. Box 2138, Santa Monica, CA 90407-2138
1200 South Hayes Street, Arlington, VA 22202-5050
201 North Craig Street, Suite 202, Pittsburgh, PA 15213-1516
RAND URL: http://www.rand.org/
To order RAND documents or to obtain additional information, contact
Distribution Services: Telephone: (310) 451-7002;
Fax: (310) 451-6915; Email: order@rand.org

Preface

Protecting the American homeland is now a critical priority for the nation, and steps are under way to improve the capabilities of civilian organizations throughout the country. The role of the U.S. military, and especially the Army, is to be prepared to make up for any deficiencies in these capabilities, as it has in domestic emergencies throughout our history. Since the 2001 terrorist attacks against the World Trade Center and the Pentagon, the Army has taken critical steps to improve its capabilities for homeland security (HLS). The question is whether more should be done to hedge against the risk that these capabilities may not be sufficient, given future dangers and risks.

This report explores ways in which the Army in both its active and reserve components could respond today by conducting more-specialized HLS training, by improving its responsiveness for domestic emergencies, and/or by augmenting certain types of its capabilities and then suggests a hedging strategy the Army could adopt. This report would be of interest to anyone concerned with how the nation will defend itself against terrorism and the U.S. Army's role in that defense.

In the Army, this research was sponsored by the Deputy Chief of Staff for Operations and Plans (G-3). It was conducted in the RAND Arroyo Center's Strategy, Doctrine, and Resources Program. The Arroyo Center is a federally funded research and development center sponsored by the U.S. Army.

Contents

Figures

Tables

Summary

The Army has played a critical role historically in ensuring the nation's security at home and can expect to be called on in the future to counter terrorist attacks and respond to other types of domestic emergencies. While the nation places primary and immediate responsibility for homeland security (HLS) with civilian organizations and the National Guard working for the state governors, the Army must be prepared to make up for any deficiencies.

The Army has taken a number of steps to improve its planning and capabilities for HLS, which is defined in this report to be activities in support of civilian organizations in domestic emergencies, including terrorist attacks, natural disasters, and civil disturbances.[1]

This report explores whether the Army should do more to hedge against the risks of being inadequately prepared for HLS tasks, given a world where terrorists have demonstrated the willingness and capability to conduct mass-casualty attacks within the United States and where the capabilities of civilian law enforcement agencies and emergency responders are expanding but still untested.

To do this, we designed a hybrid approach to dealing with HLS's uncertainties and the Army's requirements—one that focuses on possibilities against which the Army might wish to hedge. The possibilities were based on different assumptions about the character-

---

[1] Our definition encompasses what the Department of Defense calls Civil Support missions: Military Assistance to Civil Authorities (MACA), Military Assistance for Civil Disturbances (MACDIS), and Military Support to Civilian Law Enforcement Agencies (MSCLEA). See DoD (2004).

istics and seriousness of the terrorist threat, the adequacy of the capabilities of civilian organizations, and the nature of competing demands on Army forces overseas. The possibilities are theoretical, and in no way are we suggesting that they will happen. Rather, we suggest that they are plausible and could result in serious risks to the nation if they were to occur.

The approach goes on to define ways in which the Army could prepare *today,* by conducting more-specialized training, by improving its responsiveness, and/or by augmenting certain types of its capabilities. Table S.1 describes the five theoretical possibilities we explored and illustrative Army responses. Figure S.1 describes the HLS benefits of each of the Army responses.

Obviously, the Army would take such steps—if they were cost-free. But this is not the case. All of the potential Army responses involve costs, including the costs of raising or not raising the Army's

Table S.1
HLS Possibilities and Illustrative Army Responses

Possibility	Illustrative Army Response
National Guard is not adequately prepared, because of focus on conventional wars	Improve National Guard's HLS capabilities by providing DoD Title 32 funding and improved sharing of state assets
Active-duty component (AC) is not available quickly enough or adequately trained to respond to large-scale domestic emergencies	Dedicate brigade for rapid reaction, rotating between AC and National Guard (3,600 soldiers)
Law enforcement combined with available Army counterterrorism capabilities cannot meet demands of future terrorist attacks	Create rapidly deployable and dedicated AC combating terrorism force (6,200 soldiers)
AC cannot respond adequately to large-scale domestic emergencies, because significant numbers are deployed overseas	Give National Guard primary responsibility for HLS activities by creating dedicated rapid-response regional civil support battalions (8,900 soldiers)
Units critical for HLS in U.S. Army Reserve (USAR) are not available because they are deployed overseas, not ready quickly enough, and prohibited by statute from conducting all missions	Dedicate pool of USAR units to exclusive HLS mission (7,560 soldiers)

manpower caps, the costs to the Army's other missions, financial costs, and costs in the form of provoking political resistance (see Table S.2). Financial costs would be higher than Table S.2 suggests if the Army's manpower caps were raised.

What emerges from our analysis is that adopting any steps to improve the Army's HLS capabilities would result in *certain* costs

Figure S.1
HLS Benefits of Army Responses

Response	Benefits				How Accomplished	
	HLS units are...			AC Overseas Readiness	Force Structure	Planning
	More responsive	Available	Specially trained			
Army National Guard Training			X			
AC/Army National Guard HLS Ready Brigade	X	X	X			
AC/Combating Terrorism Force	X	X	X			
Army National Guard Primary HLS Responsibility	X	X	X	X		
Dedicate Rapid USAR Units	X	X	X	X		

RAND *MG221-3.1*

Table S.2
Estimated Costs of Illustrative Army Responses
($ Millions)

Army Response	Startup Costs	Annual Costs
Army National Guard Training	0	20
AC/Army National Guard HLS Ready Brigade	0	200
Combating Terrorism Force	1,000 to 1,400	0
Army National Guard Primary HLS Responsibility	400 to 600	0
Dedicate Rapid USAR Units	0	0

NOTE: Assumes no changes in Army end strength.

today, with only the *promise of benefits* in the future were any of these HLS possibilities actually to arise. Without being able to predict the future, the choice for the nation then is what kinds of HLS risks it is willing to assume and whether to undertake a hedging strategy.

Based on our analysis, a multifaceted hedging strategy on the part of the Army could make sense.

- First, given the National Guard's responsibility and availability to respond to domestic emergencies, the Army should support legislation that would make it possible for the Department of Defense (DoD) to fund HLS activities and for the National Guard to share its resources more easily across state borders. The Army should also seek the necessary statutory changes so that the USAR can conduct all HLS missions, including responses to natural disasters.
- Second, given the possibility that units in all components of the Army may be unavailable because of deployments overseas and the need already acknowledged by DoD for units in all of the Army's components to be ready and on alert, the Army should take the additional step of dedicating some forces to HLS emergencies, making them ready for rapid deployment and ensuring that they are appropriately trained.
- Third, because the prospective capabilities and deficiencies of civilian organizations are so uncertain, the Army should hedge again by dedicating a mix of forces for HLS with some units trained in specialized law enforcement capabilities.
- Fourth, the dedicated units should be drawn from the National Guard to permit the active-duty Army and supporting USAR units to be available for deployments overseas and to capitalize on the Guard's historical experiences in domestic emergencies and links to state and local emergency responders. To be effective as a hedge, the National Guard would need to create standing regional HLS task forces across the country, with units dedicated and trained for HLS and with capabilities for rapid response.

What is needed is for the nation to decide that it is worth bearing the costs today that are associated with the Army becoming better prepared for HLS than it presently is (in the aftermath of September 11) in order to *hedge* against a future that is uncertain, but one that could involve serious risks if the Army were found unprepared.

Acknowledgments

This report benefited from the support and assistance we received from many people in the Army. In particular, we thank Colonel Ken Stilley of the California Army National Guard and Donna Barbisch. Our understanding of legal differences between the various components of the Army was greatly enhanced by conversations we had with Major General Timothy Lowenberg, the Adjutant General for the State of Washington. We also thank several people at the National Guard Bureau, including Colonel David Germain, Lieutenant Colonel Gregory Wilmoth, Major Mark Bauer, USAF, and Charles Sines. The study also benefited from the insights gained from Lieutenant Don Wodash, the plans, operations, and military support officer for the State of Arizona, and Lieutenant Colonel Matthew Buretz from the Office of the Chief of Army Reserves.

Our colleagues at RAND, past and present, also provided invaluable assistance: Frances Lussier, Lieutenant Colonel Scott O'Neil, Lieutenant Colonel Stephen Dalzell, Mike Duval, David Howell, and Miranda Priebe. We especially appreciated the support and counsel throughout our project of our Arroyo Center program director, Lauri Zeman. This report also benefited from the insightful comments and suggestions of our RAND reviewers, Roger Brown and Brian Rosen, and of our outside reviewer Michele A. Flournoy. We also thank Dan Sheehan for his careful and thoughtful editing of our report and Michele Guemes for shepherding our report through the RAND publication process. The content and conclusions of the report, however, remain solely the responsibility of the authors.

Abbreviations

AC	Active component
AGR	Active Guard and Reserve
CAAP	Critical Asset Assurance Program
CBIRF	Chemical-Biological Incident Response Force
CBRNE	Chemical, Biological, Radiological, Nuclear and High Explosives
CS	Combat Support
CSB	Civil support battalion
CSS	Combat Service Support
DHS	Department of Homeland Security
DoD	Department of Defense
DRF	Division Ready Force
EMAC	Emergency Mutual Assistance Compact
FEMA	Federal Emergency Management Agency
FORSCOM	U.S. Army Forces Command
FSA	Force Structure Allowance
GMD	Ground-Based Midcourse Defense
HLS	Homeland security
IRC	Initial Ready Company
JMETL	Joint Mission-Essential Task List

JTF-CS	Joint Task Force–Civil Support
MACA	Military Assistance to Civil Authorities
MACDIS	Military Assistance for Civil Disturbances
MBEs	Mobilization Base Expansion (units)
MOS	Military Occupational Specialty
MSCA	Military Support to Civil Authorities
MSCLEA	Military Support to Civilian Law Enforcement Agencies
NORTHCOM	U.S. Northern Command
QRFs	Quick-reaction forces
RC	Reserve component
RRFs	Rapid-reaction forces
SAB	Strategic Armor Brigade
SASO	Stability and support operation
SIB	Strategic Infantry Brigade
SJFHQ	State Joint Force Headquarters
SS	Sensitive Support
STARCs	State Area Commands
TACON	Tactical Control
TO&E	Table of Organization and Equipment
USAR	U.S. Army Reserve
USARDEC	U.S. Army Research, Development, and Engineering Command
USC	U.S. Code
WMD	Weapons of mass destruction
WMD-CST	WMD–Civil Support Team

CHAPTER ONE

Introduction

Background

Considerable attention has been given to providing security for the American homeland since the terrorist attacks on the World Trade Center and the Pentagon in 2001. The President has formed a Homeland Security Council to coordinate the various federal activities and integrate them with those of state and local governments. Congress has established a new Department of Homeland Security (DHS), bringing under one roof most of the domestic agencies and offices responsible for homeland security (HLS), including border and transportation security, emergency preparedness and response, and critical infrastructure protection.[1]

A *National Security Strategy for Homeland Security* has been promulgated that lays out a comprehensive plan for fighting terrorism and establishes lines of authority and responsibilities for federal, state, and local governments (Office of Homeland Security, 2002). The President's budget for HLS in 2004 has more than doubled since 2002, with priority being given to improving the capabilities of civilian organizations to respond to terrorist attacks (White House, 2003, pp. 9–14). The Department of Defense (DoD) has stated that defending the nation is the U.S. military's highest priority and taken a number of steps to increase its capabilities, including the creation of U.S. Northern Command (NORTHCOM) with the missions to

---

[1] Public Law 107-296, signed November 25, 2002.

protect the United States against military attacks from overseas and to provide military assistance to civil authorities.[2]

Notwithstanding these initiatives, the U.S. military faces many challenges in providing HLS, largely because of the enormous uncertainties. The most obvious uncertainty has to do with the nature of the terrorist threat. While the prospect of attacks is serious and urgent, with the possibility of widespread and devastating effects, what terrorists will seek or be able to accomplish is unknown. Uncertainties also surround how effective civilian law enforcement agencies will be in preventing attacks and how capable civilian emergency responders will be in handling attacks. While significant funds are being directed to their preparations, lacking is any standard by which to judge their capabilities or effectiveness.

A consensus has emerged that the primary responsibility for HLS should reside with civilian organizations, supplemented as necessary with DoD resources and capabilities. While the active-duty Army and U.S. Army Reserve (USAR) can be used for HLS when required, responsibility for the initial and primary military response should be with the National Guard, working under the authority of the state governors. Indeed, federal response planning is based on escalating response capabilities from local to state to national, placing the National Guard in its state mission role most often before states request federal assistance. Precisely how this response framework will apply in the context of future homeland emergencies, however, is still another uncertainty.

The responses following the 2001 terrorist attacks in New York and Washington provide some useful lessons as to how this might be achieved. However, the attacks occurred in two of the best-prepared cities in the United States and involved conventional explosives, not

---

[2] DoD has assigned the Joint Task Force–Civil Support (JTF-CS), a standing headquarters, to NORTHCOM to plan for the use of DoD units in emergencies involving weapons of mass destruction. See http://www.northcom.mil/index.cfm?fuseaction=news.factsheets& factsheet=3. Congress has also approved a new senior DoD position, the Assistant Secretary for Homeland Defense, with authority to establish policies, procedures, and strategies for all military activities related to both homeland defense and HLS.

weapons of mass destruction (WMD). So the experiences may not be transferable to future terrorist attacks.

The challenge then for the U.S. military, and especially the Army, in HLS is to be prepared to make up any deficiencies in the capabilities of others, just as it has done in the past in serious domestic emergencies, and to do this within an environment of significant uncertainties.

By "HLS" in this report, we mean military activities in support of civilian organizations—i.e., those involved in preventing and responding to attacks from terrorist or possibly enemy irregular military forces as well as in responding to other kinds of domestic emergencies, including natural disasters and civil disturbances.[3] This is a broader definition for HLS than is found in *The National Security Strategy for Homeland Security*, which focuses only on terrorism. It encompasses what the Department of Defense calls Civil Support missions: Military Assistance to Civil Authorities (MACA), Military Assistance for Civil Disturbances (MACDIS), and Military Support to Civilian Law Enforcement Agencies (MSCLEA). We will not examine well-established counterdrug operations or those other activities DoD includes under homeland defense (military protection of the U.S. territory, the domestic population, and critical defense infrastructure against external threats and aggression) or under emergency preparedness.[4]

The Army's Role in HLS

The Army has been involved in what is now called "homeland security" for as long as the nation has existed. It has defended the borders

---

[3] In seeking to ensure adequate homeland defense capabilities, some experts are including the threat of clandestine or "irregular" military forces from enemy states, which could seek to target U.S. military power-projection sites and lines of communication. See Andrew Krepinevich (2000), available at http://www.csbaonline.org/4Publications/Archive/H.20000118.Whither_the_Army/H.20000118.Whither_the_Army.htm.

[4] For a description of these various types of HLS activities, see DoD (2004).

and supported civilian authorities during natural disasters, emergencies, insurrections, and riots when state and local resources have been overwhelmed. On almost a daily basis, some Army units are involved in these traditional HLS missions, though over the last century, protecting the nation's borders has not been a high priority, except in the case of counterdrug operations.

The National Guard is the most often involved in HLS activities, largely because it has a presence in each state and can be called up by the governor within a very short time, measured in hours or a few days. Another advantage is that the Guard is usually closely connected to the state emergency management system. In a majority of states the adjutant general heads both. Finally, Guardsmen on state active duty are not limited in their ability to conduct law enforcement, because federal statutes, including the *Posse Comitatus* Act, only pertain to the federal military.[5]

The large majority of the Army's HLS activities have been small, such as helping firefighters battle a large forest fire. Most operations involve only a small number of soldiers—perhaps a squad, platoon, or sometimes even a company. In those unusual cases when the incident is large, such as a hurricane, earthquake, or flood, governors may call to state active duty a larger portion of their National Guard forces or request Guardsmen from other states. In those very unusual cases when an incident overwhelms state civilian and National Guard resources, the President has ordered active-duty Army forces to lend support. Such incidents have been relatively infrequent: examples include Hurricane Andrew, Typhoon Iniki, and the Los Angeles riots, all in 1992; Hurricane Marilyn in 1995; Hurricane Floyd in 1999, and forest fires in the western United States in 2000. In these cases, the number of active Army soldiers ranged from several thousand to some 15,000 (Hurricane Andrew). On two of these occasions, the Los Angeles riots and Hurricane Floyd, the President also

---

[5] See the appendices in this report for a description of the Army's capabilities for HLS, for the legal issues raised for the Army in conducting HLS operations, and for the command relationships when Army forces are employed.

federalized some tens of thousands of National Guardsmen.[6] The USAR is rarely involved in HLS tasks because legal and policy restrictions require time to call its members to active duty and because Congress has limited its HLS operations to WMD or terrorist attacks that may result in significant losses of life or property.

In the immediate aftermath of the September 2001 terrorist attacks, the military supplemented the capabilities of the police, fire departments, and medical units at both the World Trade Center and the Pentagon. Within 24 hours, the New York National Guard had more than 4,000 soldiers on active duty, with some 1,000 providing security, medical, and engineering services. The military also took immediate steps to provide security against further attacks in the skies and around critical government facilities. In the ensuing weeks, some 7,000 Army Reserve soldiers were called up to provide rescue support, civil engineers, communication and power-generation systems, medical teams, and other service support operations—e.g., food and shelter. Soon after the attacks, the National Guard, under the control of the state governors, provided security at more than 400 airports. The National Guard and others in the Army also supplemented civilian efforts in providing security of the nation's borders, seaports, bridges, power plants, and government buildings as well as at such special events as the Winter Olympics (Davis and Shapiro, 2003, pp. 67–69).

Although the Army has unique capabilities, it is called on for the most part in domestic emergencies because it can provide an organized pool of labor and equipment and, in exceptional circumstances, it can employ forces to maintain order and assist in the enforcement of state and federal laws. The Army's approach to HLS has, therefore, been to rely on active and reserve forces that have been sized, orga-

---

[6] Background on Army responses can be found for the Los Angeles riots (Delk, 1995; Los Angeles Board of Police Commissioners, 1992; and Schnaubelt, 1997, pp. 88–109) and for Hurricane Andrew (McDonnell, 1993).

nized, trained, and equipped to fight wars, essentially treating HLS as a lesser included case.[7]

Over the past few years, the Army has, however, taken some critical steps to improve its HLS capabilities. At congressional urging, the Army is creating in the National Guard special teams to respond to incidents involving WMD. They are called Weapons of Mass Destruction–Civil Support Teams (WMD-CSTs). Fifty-five teams are currently planned and at least one will be deployed in each of the states and territories. They are each manned by 22 full-time National Guardsmen. While they will be federally funded and trained, they will normally perform their mission under the command and control of the state governors.[8] The Army is also in the process of creating the Guardian Brigade from existing units, with a headquarters element and trained personnel, to provide a specialized and tailored response force in the event of an attack involving the use of WMD at home or overseas.[9]

Within the active component (AC), the Army as part of its transformation is increasing from 33 active brigades to 43 modular active brigade units of action and restructuring to provide more high-demand capabilities, such as military police and special operations forces.[10] Both of these steps will make the active Army more responsive not only to overseas contingencies but also to emergencies at home.

The Army has developed plans to provide headquarters elements to assist local, state, and federal civilian agencies and provide com-

---

[7] For an analysis of what the Army has been called on to do until the mid-1990s, see Brown, Fedorochko, and Schank (1995). The authors concluded that there was no basis for sizing the Army for domestic emergencies.

[8] For a description of these WMD-CSTs, see DoD (2003c).

[9] See USARDEC (2003).

[10] See testimony of Lieutenant General Richard A. Cody, Deputy Chief of Staff, G-3, and Lieutenant General Franklin L. Hagenbeck, Deputy Chief of Staff, G-1, before U.S. House of Representatives, Committee on Armed Services, Subcommittee on Total Force, March 10, 2004.

mand and control of military units responding to HLS emergencies.[11] It has also designated certain active Army units, on a rotating basis, to be on heightened alert for HLS emergencies (Burns, 2003). Two brigades are being maintained to respond to potential actions involving military assistance to civil disturbances in accordance with the DoD Civil Disturbance Plan (DoD, 2003c, p. 5). In addition, five battalions are designated to provide rapid-reaction forces (RRFs) and quick-reaction forces (QRFs) for HLS emergencies, such as critical infrastructure protection, counterterrorism operations, and consequence management (DoD, 2003c, p. 5).[12] The existence of this capability was highlighted in recent DoD reports and testimony, but neither the size of the units nor the speed of deployment was specified. That being said, however, it is likely given past Army practice that an RRF is a battalion that has an 18-hour deployment window, and a QRF is a platoon or company with a deployment window of two to four hours.[13] In both of these cases, the units do not have any specialized training for HLS and are available for deployment to an overseas contingency. If deployed for an HLS contingency, these units would serve under the operational control of NORTHCOM.

---

[11] The First and Fifth Continental Armies are responsible for activating and deploying a Response Task Force to provide the command and control. The Army has been directed to assume the role of Joint Task Force–East and Joint Task Force–West, respectively, to provide support for all ground forces supporting a lead federal agency. See http://www.army.mil/2003TransformationRoadmap/Chapt6.pdf.

[12] See also Burns (2003) and testimony of the Joint Chiefs of Staff before the Committee on Armed Services, U.S. House of Representatives, February 4, 2004.

[13] For decades the Army has maintained alert brigades that are capable of rapid deployment. The lead battalion within the alert brigade is called the Division Ready Force (DRF) and must be prepared to begin deployment within 18 hours of notification. The lead company of the DRF may also be designated as the Initial Ready Company (IRC). The IRC historically has been locked in to the company barracks to ensure that it is ready to deploy within four hours of notification. At times, the IRC has been given a mission to be the first unit to respond during civil disturbances. This model has served the Army well for both rapid overseas deployments and civil disturbances and has likely been adapted to meet new requirements within the United States. For an unclassified discussion of the Division Ready Brigade, see http://globalsecurity.org/military/agency/army/drb.htm. This Web site also contains a description of the DRF, QRF, and IRC. Although the discussion of the QRF is not specific to HLS, the size and response time of the unit is most likely representative of the units on alert within the United States.

In the National Guard, rapid-reaction forces are being planned for every state and territory to handle various types of HLS emergencies. They would deploy as state militia in support of their governors. The National Guard has also consolidated its headquarter organizations in each state into a Standing Joint Force Headquarters, which provides for rapid response within the state and the integration of activities across states through Emergency Mutual Assistance Compacts (EMACs) (Blum, 2004). These EMACs offer a quick and easy way for states to send equipment and personnel to assist in emergencies in other states and provide a legally binding contractual arrangement that makes the requesting state responsible for all costs of out-of-state forces.[14] So far, every state but California and two of the four territories have either ratified the EMACs or are in the process of doing so.

The USAR, which has critical types of units for HLS, is also being reorganized to enhance its capability to respond quickly for emergency missions at home or overseas. Units will be placed on a 96–120 hour alert status for six- to nine-month periods (Helmly, 2004).

Outside Groups' Recommendations for Additional Army Steps

Recognizing the critical role that the Army plays in HLS and the new challenges it faces, a few commissions and study groups outside government have offered recommendations for further steps the Army should take. They tend to give the primary role for HLS to the Guard and Reserve and to call for a shift in the priorities of the National Guard away from conventional warfare. Where they differ is in how this should be done.

The Hart-Rudman Commission in 2001 recommended that "the Secretary of Defense, at the president's direction, should make

---

[14] U.S. Public Law 104-321, October 19, 1996.

HLS a primary mission of the National Guard, and the Guard should be organized, properly trained, and adequately equipped to undertake that mission. . . . The National Guard should redistribute resources currently allocated predominantly to preparing for conventional wars overseas to provide greater support to civil authorities in preparing for and responding to disasters, especially emergencies involving weapons of mass destruction" (U.S. Commission on National Security/21st Century, 2001, p. 24). The commission did not, however, describe what specific changes should be made.

The Gilmore Commission, in its 2002 report, made a number of recommendations to improve the nation's military capabilities for HLS. Given "the possibility of a major attack on U.S. soil of a size that would overwhelm even the best-prepared cities," the commission recommended that "the Combatant Commander, NORTHCOM, have dedicated, rapid-reaction units with a wide range of response capabilities, such as the ability to support implementation of a quarantine, support crowd control activities, provide CBRNE [Chemical, Biological, Radiological, Nuclear, and High Explosives] detection and decontamination, provide emergency medical response, perform engineering, and provide communication support to and among the leadership of civil authorities in the event of a terrorist attack." It then suggested that the force could be drawn from any part of the Army but should involve such capabilities as military police, command and control, medical, engineering, CBRNE detection/decontamination, and liaison elements (Advisory Panel to Assess Domestic Response Capabilities for Terrorism Involving Weapons of Mass Destruction, 2002, pp. 99–101).

The Gilmore Commission further recommended that the National Guard's civil support capability be enhanced by assigning certain units HLS as their "exclusive mission" and by giving them sufficient training and resources. This is a change in the commission's earlier recommendation, which called for the National Guard to be assigned HLS missions "as their primary missions with combat missions outside the United States as secondary missions" (Advisory Panel to Assess Domestic Response Capabilities for Terrorism Involving Weapons of Mass Destruction, 2002, p. 103).

The Heritage Foundation Homeland Security Task Force called for freeing up the National Guard and Reserve for HLS. In the task force's view, this should be done by providing additional combat support and combat service support in the active forces, by increasing the number of active-duty personnel, and by ensuring that the National Guard has standing emergency plans to train and work with local authorities on homeland defense and consequence management (Bremer and Meese, 2002, p. 9).

Should the Army Do More?

The question for the nation then is whether the Army should do more to prepare for HLS activities to hedge against the risk of being inadequately prepared, given a world where terrorists have demonstrated the willingness and capability to conduct mass-casualty attacks within the United States and where civilian capabilities are expanding but still untested.

To answer this question, this report adopts an approach, described in Chapter Two, that begins with theoretical HLS possibilities involving terrorist attacks, civil disturbances, and other types of domestic emergencies that could require responses that would overwhelm both civilian organizations and the Army's available capabilities. It then defines ways in which the Army could respond *today,* by conducting more-specialized training, by improving its responsiveness, and/or by augmenting certain types of its capabilities.

The five theoretical possibilities and illustrative Army responses are described in Chapter Three. In Chapter Four, the report evaluates these Army responses in terms of their financial, opportunity, and political costs. This sets the stage for recommendations in the final chapter for steps the Army should take to become better prepared for HLS to hedge against a future that is uncertain but could involve serious risks to the nation if the Army were found unprepared.

CHAPTER TWO

A Hedging Approach to Future Homeland Security Risks

Any effort to define the Army's requirements for HLS must deal with many uncertainties. Some of these are similar to those defense planners have confronted in the past, such as uncertainties about the nature of the threat. In the case of HLS, debate continues on what kinds of attacks might be undertaken and what are the prospects for terrorists to acquire different kinds of capabilities. Other uncertainties are unique to the Army's role in HLS, such as those involving the potential shortfalls that may emerge in civilian capabilities that the Army could be called on to fill.

The Army, in line with DoD's capabilities-based approach, has units of different kinds ready for HLS activities, though most of these are also available for contingencies overseas. It has not established specific or separate requirements for HLS.

RAND studies in the past have sought to define the Army's HLS requirements by relying on historical Army experiences in various types of domestic emergencies and then extrapolating from these to define responses to potential terrorist attack scenarios involving conventional, chemical, biological, and radiological weapons. In one RAND study, the authors concluded by defining a range of possible Army HLS requirements, based on the Army's current commitments to the homeland security missions and estimates of the possible surge requirements. (RAND Arroyo Center, 2002, pp. 24–28; Larson and Peters, 2001). In another, after defining ways to estimate requirements for each of six potential Army homeland security tasks, the study concluded by calling for the Army to have capabilities for responses that were quick and large (thereby requiring active Army units) as well as capabilities for long-term responses (where the reserves could be used) (Davis, 2003, pp. 61–83).

These studies did not, however, produce a specific set of Army requirements for homeland security for reasons that are not too surprising. A variety of terrorist attack scenarios can be defined, but the uncertainties make it difficult to choose any one or even a few of these as a basis for future Army planning. Natural disasters will occur, but their timing, location, and effects also remain uncertain. Information can be collected on past Army responses to HLS emergencies, but such experiences may not be relevant in a future where terrorist attacks could involve widespread biological or radiological contamination or be multiple and simultaneous. The Army may also lack the same kinds of Stateside capabilities it had in the past, given the recurring demands on all the Army's components for overseas deployments. Finally, the capabilities and response time of local, state, and federal civilian organizations will increase, thereby reducing in unknown ways potential Army requirements.

To address the central question in this report of whether the Army should do more to hedge against the risk that it could find itself inadequately prepared for terrorism and other domestic emergencies, we turned to methodologies RAND has developed in the past to help defense planners deal with risk and uncertainty.

One of these is the assumption-based planning methodology. Rather than starting with what is known and trying to predict the future, it uses as its point of departure the assumptions that underlie any given strategy and looks for ways these could become vulnerable. It then calls for defining signposts that indicate the changing vulnerability of an assumption, shaping actions to avert a vulnerable assumption, and hedging actions to better prepare an organization for the failure of one of its important assumptions (Dewar et al., 1993).

Another RAND defense planning methodology "takes *a decision perspective*, which focuses research . . . on issues central to potential decisions, rather than searching for knowledge generally. Also, it recognizes that to serve decision needs, some matters must be understood in both breadth and depth, and the key issue of risk must be understood so that it can be reduced." According to the authors, the approach is in the spirit of capabilities-based planning (Davis, Bigelow, and McEver, 1999). Still another RAND planning methodology, the "strategies-to-tasks methodology," is designed to provide an audit train from the broadest strategic objectives down to operational activities at the tactical level, which among uses can help identify gaps in capability (Thaler, 1993; Kent and Ochmanek, 2003).

Drawing then on these defense planning methodologies as well as RAND's earlier substantive analyses of HLS requirements, we developed what might be viewed as a hybrid approach to dealing with HLS's uncertainties and the Army's requirements, one that focuses on possibilities against which the Army might wish to hedge.

The approach begins by postulating five possibilities in which civilian agencies and the Army could find themselves unable to adequately address HLS needs. The possibilities were designed based on different assumptions about the characteristics and seriousness of the terrorist threat, the adequacy of the capabilities of civilian organizations, and the nature of competing demands on Army forces overseas.

The possibilities are theoretical. We are in no way suggesting that any of these will actually happen but rather that they are plausible and could result in serious risks to the nation if the Army were not adequately prepared. They are neither the only possibilities that could arise in the future nor are they mutually exclusive.

For each of the possibilities, we designed a response the Army could take *today* to become better prepared through changes in its current planning, force structure, or training. For those responses involving force structure changes, an illustrative force structure was defined based on the Army's historical HLS experiences and the types of tasks that the Army would be required to perform in responding to the possibility.

Table 2.1 outlines possible Army HLS tasks, those that are general and those unique to responding to terrorism. Many of the general HLS tasks could be done by Army soldiers with little, if any, specialized training. What is often required is simply an organized pool of

Table 2.1
Possible Army Homeland Security Tasks

HLS Tasks: General	HLS Tasks: Responding to Terrorism
Provide organized, directed, and able-bodied labor (fill sandbags, man fire lines, etc.)	Employ intelligence, surveillance, and reconnaissance for use by civil authorities (e.g., law enforcement) to track terrorists
Provide support to law enforcement (immediate force presence and crowd and riot control; establish perimeters; man roadblocks; direct traffic; aid in evacuations; enforce quarantines, keep-out zones, and curfews; protect critical infrastructure)	Provide air defense (air- and ground-based) of high-value targets
	Augment border controls
Transport supplies and services	Provide antiterrorism and counter-terrorism support to law enforcement
Provide emergency medical care (first aid to field hospitals; medical evacuation)	Provide chemical, biological, or radiological surveillance, decon-tamination, and specialized medical support
Rescue/evacuate people (search and rescue)	
Provide engineering support (clear debris, restore public utilities, repair buildings, provide emergency power)	
Provide shelter, food, water, clothing, sanitation	
Provide linguists to disaster sites	
Provide liaison services and coordination with wider civil community	
Provide emergency mortuary services	
Provide emergency air traffic control, port operations	
Provide command and control (coordinate emergency operations; establish and maintain communications within and outside affected area; provide military intelligence, finance, public affairs, civil affairs, and adjutant general support)	

SOURCES: The general tasks are derived from the Army's responses to Hurricane Andrew and the Los Angeles riots, both in 1992, Hurricane Floyd in 1999, and the forest fires in the western United States in 2000. (See Chapter One, footnote 6.) The responses to terrorism tasks are derived from our assessment of the types of special-ized tasks that may emerge in the context of future terrorist attacks, if they occur, particularly those with WMD.

able-bodied labor. Soldiers with some limited training could do some of the support to law enforcement tasks, such as sealing off areas. Other general HLS tasks will require more specialized units: medical, engineering, civil affairs, and command and control. Finally, those relatively few tasks unique to responding to terrorism are likely to require highly trained specialists, such as those with expertise in operating in a chemical, biological, or radiological environment or in performing counterterrorism operations.

For purposes of our analysis, we have defined a single discrete Army response for each possibility, though others exist and they are not mutually exclusive. An Army hedging strategy could involve a combination of one or more of these responses. We have focused on the Army, though any future HLS operation will likely be joint in nature, involving the Air Force and possibly the Navy and Marines.

The five Army responses, by design, have benefits for the Army in its capabilities to conduct future HLS operations. At the same time, they each have costs, or they would likely have been done already. So the final step in the approach is to define the price the Army, and the nation, must pay in terms of financial, opportunity, and political costs if these responses were adopted.

CHAPTER THREE

Homeland Security Possibilities and Army Responses

The central question in this report is whether the Army should do more to hedge against the risk that it could find itself inadequately prepared for terrorism and other domestic emergencies. To answer this question, we defined five theoretical possibilities in which such a risk could arise because of a lack of the specialized training, responsiveness, or right types of units for HLS.

The possibilities are similar in that they all assume that the capabilities of civilian organizations and those in the National Guard available to state governors are overwhelmed. They differ in the characteristics of the shortfalls that emerge. Responses are then defined for ways the Army could achieve today by changing its planning, force structure, and training.

For purposes of analysis, these theoretical HLS possibilities are treated separately, though more than one could arise, and the individual Army response could be useful in more than the single possibility. Also for purposes of analysis, the Army responses do not involve the raising of the Army component manpower caps.

See Table 3.1 for a description of the five possibilities and the illustrative Army responses. While the analysis focuses on the Army responses, in many of these, support from the other armed services, particularly the Air Force for airlift, is required. These are also described.

Table 3.1
Homeland Security Possibilities and Illustrative Army Responses

Possibility	Illustrative Army Response
National Guard is not adequately prepared, because of focus on conventional wars	Improve National Guard's HLS capabilities by providing DoD Title 32 funding and improved sharing of state assets
Active-duty component (AC) is not available quickly enough or adequately trained to respond to large-scale domestic emergencies	Dedicate brigade for rapid reaction, rotating between AC and National Guard (3,600 soldiers)
Law enforcement combined with available Army counterterrorism capabilities cannot meet demands of future terrorist attacks	Create rapidly deployable and dedicated AC combating terrorism force (6,200 soldiers)
AC cannot respond adequately to large-scale domestic emergencies, because significant numbers are deployed overseas	Give National Guard primary responsibility for HLS activities by creating dedicated rapid-response regional civil support battalions (8,900 soldiers)
Units critical for HLS in USAR are not available because they are deployed overseas, not ready quickly enough, and prohibited by statute from conducting all missions	Dedicate a pool of USAR units to exclusive HLS mission (7,560 soldiers)

Improve National Guard HLS Capabilities

One homeland security possibility is that the effects of future terrorist attacks will require responses that the National Guard will be inadequately prepared to provide, given its current focus on training and preparing for conventional wars. Limits on the availability of state and federal funding as well as requirements for maintaining warfighting proficiencies mean that the National Guard often cannot undertake the types of planning and exercises necessary for its role in HLS, which will require close coordination with a variety of different civilian government agencies at the local and state level, interactions with civilian populations, and an understanding of the various statutory and regulatory authorities that govern the use of Army forces within the United States.

An Army response could be to give to the National Guard of each state a specific federal mission to be prepared to conduct HLS activities both within the state and in other states requiring assistance, to be accomplished in accordance with a mutual aid compact or as a federal response force. This would permit National Guard units to receive DoD Title 32 funding for training for HLS activities as well as for the conduct of preplanned HLS activities, such as border patrols and surveillance, exercises, and planning activities, on the request of a state governor and with the approval of the Secretary of Defense. This would be similar to how counterdrug operations are conducted today. In this response, statutory changes would also be made to permit Guardsmen, when undertaking HLS missions outside their home state, to engage in law enforcement activities and to receive federal tort protection for the large number of HLS missions for which they are not protected today.[1]

Characteristics of Response

DoD's Title 32 funds have traditionally been limited by law to training and readiness activities associated with the National Guard's warfighting mission. Since the early 1990s, however, Congress has authorized National Guard units to use Title 32 funds to conduct a wide range of counterdrug activities.[2] This Army response would create a similar program for federal funding of training and preplanned, scheduled HLS operations.[3] The amount each state would receive would depend on the needs of the state as specified by the governor

---

[1] Federal tort protection is afforded to all National Guardsmen who are federalized—i.e., operating in Title 10 status. Members of the National Guard are also extended federal tort protections in some specific circumstances under Title 32 status, as specified in 28 USC 2671 and 2679. Federal tort protection for Guardsmen in Title 32 status includes such duties as monthly drill, annual training, attendance at service schools, and specified drug interdiction activities. Note, however, that these are specifically delineated aspects of federal tort protection, which would not apply to a broad range of HLS activities under the current statute. See 28 USC 2671, extending federal tort protection to members of the National Guard who are operating pursuant to 32 USC 115, 316, 502, 503, 504, or 505.

[2] The National Guard's responsibilities in drug interdiction and counterdrug activities are specified in 32 USC 112 (2003).

[3] The unsuccessful "Feinstein Amendment" to the Homeland Security Act of 2002 (Public Law 107-296) would have established funding and assistance for National Guard HLS activities similar to what is being proposed in this option but would not have addressed tort protection issues.

and both verified and approved by the Secretary of Defense. The costs associated with HLS operations in an emergency would be paid as today by the requesting state, Title 32 funds, or Title 10 funds, if the unit were federalized.

Congress would authorize the Secretary of Defense to provide funds to the governor of a state after the submission of an HLS activities plan that specifies how personnel, equipment, and training facilities will be used. This response does not assume that the units would require any unique, expensive equipment for carrying out HLS activities. The plan would provide a detailed explanation of why the National Guard is needed to perform the specified activities as well as a certification that the activities are consistent with their state laws and serve state law enforcement or other emergency response purposes.[4]

The funds could be used for pay, allowances, clothing, subsistence and travel, and related expenses; for operations and maintenance of equipment and facilities; and for the procurement of services and the leasing of equipment. To ensure that minimum standards result from the training program, DoD and/or DHS would establish individual and unit standards and develop course materials for meeting those standards.

This response would also make it easier for states to share National Guard assets on state active-duty status for HLS missions. This would be done by ensuring the uniformity of state laws and extending tort protections to all National Guardsmen. In other words, those members of the National Guard conducting HLS activities in other states would have the same powers, privileges, and immunities of National Guard forces of the requesting state.

In addition, to give governors more flexibility in sharing forces, this response would authorize the states to enter into mutual assistance compacts for enforcing state laws, protecting critical infrastructure, and other HLS activities currently prohibited. While the current EMAC allows the National Guard to respond to natural and man-

---

[4] These requirements are similar to those that apply for Title 32 funding for National Guard counterdrug operations today, pursuant to 32 USC 112.

made disasters in other states while remaining in state active-duty status, it specifically prohibits the use of out-of-state units for important HLS missions that might involve the arrest of an individual violating state or federal law or for any mission that the President is authorized to federalize the National Guard.[5]

Training

National Guard units would conduct training for HLS based on the specific requirements articulated by the governor's HLS activity plan. All HLS training conducted pursuant to this plan would be in addition to the training required by the National Guard to remain adequately prepared for its federal warfighting requirement. To reduce the burden on Guardsmen, the HLS training would be done by units, using volunteers if available, designated by the states to be their first-responding units or those entering their individual and small-unit training cycle. As much of the training as possible would be done through distance learning because the needed skills involve familiarity with plans, laws, and procedures necessary to support civil authorities. Officers and senior enlisted Guardsmen would conduct staff exercises with their key state counterparts and with NORTHCOM.

Legal Issues

This response would require three statutory changes. First, it would require authorizing the use of DoD Title 32 funds and providing for DoD oversight of HLS activities conducted as part of this program. The EMAC (as codified by Public Law 104-321) also must be modified to allow members of the National Guard to conduct operations

---

[5] Public Law 104-321, the Emergency Mutual Assistance Compact (EMAC), was signed into law on October 19, 1996. Article XIII of the EMAC states: "Nothing in this compact shall authorize or permit the use of military force by the national guard of a state at any place outside that state in any emergency for which the president is authorized by law to call into federal service the militia, or for any purpose for which the use of the army or the air force would in the absence of express statutory authorization be prohibited under 18 U.S.C. Sec. 1385." In essence, the existing EMAC prohibits the use of the National Guard from other states for quelling civil disturbances, insurrection, or any homeland defense mission. It also specifies that the *Posse Comitatus* Act applies to members of the National Guard from adjacent states (18 USC Sec. 1385).

associated with critical infrastructure protection, civil disturbance, or other homeland defense missions. Third, while federal statutes provide federal tort protections to members of the National Guard conducting certain Title 32 activities outside of their home states, these statutes would be expanded to include the full range of HLS training and activities. Nothing in this response would change the authority of a National Guard unit to perform law enforcement functions within its home state that it is authorized to perform by state law. Neither would this response change the limits involved in any federal Title 10 service.

Command and Control

While under state control, National Guard forces remain under the command of the adjutant general of their home state or his designated representative. National Guard units from sending states would remain under the command of their home adjutant general while being placed under the operational control of the adjutant general of the receiving state. The commander of NORTHCOM would exercise coordination authority over all military units that provide direct support to the states, DHS, or other federal agencies.[6]

Create a Dedicated Rapid-Reaction Brigade

A second homeland security possibility is that the consequences of terrorist attacks would quickly overwhelm civilian emergency responders along with the National Guard forces available to state governors, and the active-duty Army in the United States would not be available *quickly* enough or *adequately trained* to respond. From recent experiences, including responses to Hurricane Andrew and the 2001 World Trade Center attacks, the National Guard can mobilize thousands of soldiers within the first day or so of an emergency, but future terrorist attacks, especially those involving WMD, could call

---

[6] Appendix C provides more detail on these command relationships.

for many more to arrive very quickly with robust command and control and with skills in interacting with many different civilian organizations.

An Army response could be to establish a dedicated brigade-size national rapid-reaction force that would be trained for basic HLS tasks, such as sealing off areas in support of law enforcement agencies, crowd control, search and rescue, and infrastructure protection. The brigade would have an exclusive HLS mission, so that it would be always available. It would be able to respond very rapidly, the first company able to deploy within four hours, and the lead battalion of roughly 600 soldiers would deploy within 18 hours. Although the rapid-response brigade would not be large enough to handle the largest HLS scenarios, it would be the first federal force to arrive and, with its large headquarters element, it could provide command and control for all subsequent forces on the scene.

The brigade would be drawn from active-duty and National Guard units who rotate as the ready brigade, modeled on recent overseas deployments to Bosnia and Kosovo.[7] This response provides a dedicated capability for HLS without permanently devoting an active-duty unit to it. No changes in the personnel strength ceiling of either the active Army or the reserve components would be required. The brigade would replace the current active post–September 11 RRFs and QRFs, who have no specialized HLS training and can be called on for overseas deployments.

Characteristics of Response

In this Army response, an active or reserve combat brigade would be augmented in order to be relatively self-sufficient with its share of division support units, including engineers, artillery, air defense, communications, wheeled reconnaissance, a forward support battalion, a main support company, a platoon of military police, and an assault helicopter company for lift (see Table 3.2). A few corps and echelon-above-corps assets, specifically military police and civil affairs

---

[7] As the Army introduces modularity into its warfighting capabilities, the brigade in this Army response would be what is called a Unit of Action (UA).

companies, would supplement this enhanced brigade. The artillery battalion would be deployed as general-purpose soldiers (riflemen) without their major combat systems, and the air defense company would be deployed in a similar way or as air defense, depending on the situation. Both those units would receive training to emphasize their skills as soldiers and for HLS. Altogether, the enhanced brigade would be composed of roughly 3,600 soldiers and spend three to six months in ready status for HLS missions.[8]

During its rotation, the HLS ready brigade would be a Title 10 force apportioned to NORTHCOM, which, in turn, would be responsible for establishing specific HLS training requirements and

Table 3.2
Illustrative Rapid-Reaction Brigade Force Structure

Unit Type	Strength
Light Infantry Brigade (Three Battalions)	1,655
Division Support Units for Light Brigade	
Engineering Battalion	292
Artillery Battalion and Headquarters	450
Communications Company	229
Wheeled Reconnaissance Company	105
Military Police Platoon	28
Air Defense Company	150
Assault Helicopter Company	130
Forward Support Battalion	171
Main Support Company	230
Total, Brigade Support	1,785
Military Police Company	177
Civil Affairs Company	20
Total	3,637

SOURCES: RAND, based on the Army TO&E, 1999, and the MFORCE database, 2001.
NOTE: The data are based on a brigade of a light division and its support slice from the division. These numbers should be treated as illustrative because every division is structured differently.

---

[8] In creating this notional force and all the other notional forces in this report, we have used Table of Organization and Equipment (TO&E) data for existing units that perform similar functions and have relevant capabilities.

certification standards,[9] planning for potential HLS activities, and exercising operational control when they were deployed.

One of the three battalions in the brigade would be on alert, ready to deploy quickly. The first company of that brigade (the initial ready company with up to 200 soldiers) would be able to leave the installation by road or air within four hours of receiving an order to do so. It could be on the ground anywhere within the United States several hours after that, depending on transit time. The entire first battalion (roughly 600 soldiers) would be ready to deploy within 18 hours. The second battalion would follow quickly, deploying within several days of the event. The third battalion would help the others deploy and then deploy itself. It could be deployed within a week of the event.

The specific timeline for deployment would be tied to the location of the incident as well as the availability of air and ground transportation resources. The deployment of this unit would be preplanned as a contingency operation and, consequently, would have the same level of air and ground transportation priority as the existing ready brigades do. Air Force aircraft would be available based on the level of national priority established for the specific mission. In the event that Air Force assets were not appropriate for the situation or available because of other, higher-priority missions, a combination of organic ground transportation, division and corps transportation resources, and contract transportation could be drawn on to enable the units to respond, but perhaps not as quickly.

One way, but not the only way, to organize the brigade would be to rotate after four weeks the battalions standing ready to reduce the strain on the soldiers of not being allowed to leave the installation, etc. By the end of three months, each battalion would have had a turn being the ready battalion. The rotation patterns and deploy-

---

[9] NORTHCOM would identify training requirements through the development of the Joint Mission-Essential Task List (JMETL) it provides to the joint staff. As with any other Army mission, specific individual and unit training standards and training certification would be conducted by U.S. Forces Command, acting in its Title 10 capacity for the Department of the Army.

ment times assumed in this response for companies, battalions, and brigades are similar to what the Army uses for ready brigades.

The brigade (plus essential division- and corps-level assets) would spend its three- to six-month rotation in the United States at its home installation (for active component units) or mobilization station (for reserve component units) as the ready force for HLS. During that time, the brigade would do further training appropriate to its HLS mission as well as its traditional warfighting missions. After its rotation as the HLS ready brigade, it would return to its regular peacetime status. Active component units would go off alert and train for upcoming missions. Reserve component units would be demobilized and return to drilling status. Using this approach and three-month rotations would provide a full-time HLS brigade year round as long as the Army dedicated at least four brigades each year. If a brigade is on alert for more than three months, the number of brigades that would be affected each year would be reduced, but the length of their commitment would be increased.

Because most HLS missions are likely to require light, easily transportable forces, infantry units would be the most natural fit. The need to transport the forces and their equipment quickly also makes light forces a good choice. Given the other demands for light forces, however, the HLS ready brigade might need to depend on heavier forces. Whatever the type of unit, it would probably not have as much mobility as could be needed for HLS missions. Ideally, the units would be able to fall in on Humvees and trucks located close to the emergency, but this requires preplanning and may not always be available. Regardless of the type of unit, soldiers would be deployed as riflemen, leaving behind all tracked vehicles and heavy weapons. This type of deployment is the same as what is now envisioned for units assigned the QRF and RRF mission.

Training

Training is an important element of this response. Soldiers would be trained to operate in an environment where civilians are prevalent, and they will have to defer to civil authorities. The advantages of learning these skills are twofold. First, it would prepare the soldiers for HLS missions. Second, some of the skills learned for HLS would also be applicable for peacekeeping and other so-called stability and support operations (SASOs) overseas that both active and reserve component units are increasingly called on to perform.

Units assigned to the HLS mission would need to receive individual and unit-level training before they begin their assignment. For active component units, this training could take place in the months leading up to the mission. Guard units would also require time to prepare. Based on the experience of preparing Guard units for Bosnia rotations, most of the individual and collective training would be completed at their home station during the regular drilling periods in the months prior to call-up.[10] After call-up, the units would report to a mobilization center where they would receive standard and specialized training. It would take about four weeks of training before the forces would be able to assume their HLS mission, which they would perform while at their mobilization center. During its HLS assignment, the brigade could continue training. In total, it would be on active duty for about a month longer than the time of its rotation.

Legal Issues

No changes in any laws would be necessary in this response, as the units in the HLS ready brigade would be in Title 10 status.

Command and Control

The command and control relationships for the HLS ready brigade would be relatively straightforward because it would be in Title 10 status. The brigade would be assigned to U.S. Army Forces Command and through it to the Joint Forces Command. For the HLS rotation, the brigade would be placed under the operational control of NORTHCOM. After the rotation is complete, operational control of the brigade would return to the command responsible for it during peacetime.

---

[10] The scheduling data for reserve component forces are taken from U.S. Army (1999).

Provide Rapid and Dedicated Combating Terrorism Force

A third HLS possibility is that future attacks by terrorists will place demands on civilian law enforcement agencies that they cannot meet. Law enforcement agencies face the expanding need to detect terrorist networks and apprehend suspects and to do this throughout the United States and along U.S. borders. Three different types of deficiencies could arise. First, they might not have the manpower and equipment to seal off large areas where terrorists or other enemies were suspected of operating. Second, they might not have the specialized communication and other kinds of equipment needed to locate terrorists. Finally, civilian law enforcement personnel might not have the necessary capabilities to neutralize threats involving chemical, biological, radiological, or nuclear weapons or specific threats against high-value targets—for example, those located in the nation's capital. Today, highly specialized military units, including those in the Army, are capable of conducting such operations within the United States, but in this possibility they are unavailable because of their deployment overseas.[11]

An Army response could be to dedicate a portion of the active force structure to provide the nucleus of a rapidly deployable terrorism-combating force capable of conducting antiterrorism and counterterrorism activities. The organization would be designed to augment civilian law enforcement efforts quickly with highly trained and specialized forces capable of protecting critical infrastructure, providing assistance in the event of civil disturbances and area security during searches for terrorists, tracking terrorists and their weapons, and performing other antiterrorism and counterterrorism operations. It would also be available to conduct antiterrorism and counterterrorism activities on DoD installations and facilities and protect defense-related critical infrastructure.

While not capable of responding to the consequences of a large-scale emergency, this force could provide the headquarters command and control for the necessary additional units. In essence, this unit is

---

[11] Such a mission is specified in the U.S. Code, specifically USC 374, 382, and 831.

a high-end, national 911 force that would provide NORTHCOM with a capability to respond rapidly to crises with a potential law enforcement dimension without having to draw on highly trained counterterrorism units apportioned to other combatant commanders that have other worldwide missions and are already stressed by their high overseas operations tempo.

This Army response assumes that the total active Army end strength would not be increased and the soldiers would be drawn either from current combat forces or from the institutional Army. This organization would be fully capable of replacing the two brigades assigned the Military Assistance for Civil Disturbances (Garden Plot) mission as well as the QRF and RRF units in the active Army with HLS missions.

Characteristics of Response

This Army response would create a task force of some 6,200 soldiers specifically designed to support law enforcement. The organization will consist of a Task Force headquarters commanded by a major general and three independent groups, called combating terrorism groups, each commanded by a colonel. The groups would be located in different parts of the country to enable them to respond rapidly to crises that arise in their respective regions. Each group would be structured to rapidly integrate, if necessary, other specialized DoD units and capabilities, such as the Marines' Chemical-Biological Incident Response Force (CBIRF), the Army's Soldier Biological and Chemical Command's Technical Escort Unit, the Army's Chemical-Biological Rapid Response Team, the 52nd Ordnance Group (Explosive Ordnance Disposal), or the National Guard's WMD-CSTs. In addition to providing general support to law enforcement, each group would contain a small, highly trained counterterrorism force that could provide assistance to local, state, and federal law enforcement agencies when such assistance is requested by the Attorney General and authorized by the Secretary of Defense. Because of the force's unique role within the United States, DoD would train and certify members of this unit as "Department of Defense law enforcement officers." In this capacity, they would be accorded the rights and immunities of a law enforcement officer by both state and federal laws when operating within the bounds of their federal mission.

Fielding this task force would involve the creation of three combating terrorism groups, each capable of conducting independent operations within their geographic region and having a habitual relationship with the DHS regional structure as it may emerge.[12]

Specialties needed in this new organization include aviation, transportation, signal, civil affairs, military police, medical, chemical, and counterterrorism. See Table 3.3 for the types and sizes of units in each group.

Each of the three groups would be capable of conducting several small independent missions. In a large-scale incident, such as the Los Angeles riot, one or more groups could work together under the con-

Table 3.3
Illustrative Combating Terrorism Group

Unit Type	Strength
Group Headquarters	150
Military Police Battalion	580
—Three Companies	
—One Headquarters Company	
Counterterrorism Squadron	100
—Three Companies of Counterterrorism Specialists	
—One Headquarters Company	
Domestic Support Battalion	640
—Transportation Company	
—Chemical Reconnaissance/Decontamination Company	
—Signal Platoon	
—Maintenance Company	
—Civil Affairs Platoon	
—Military Intelligence Company	
Aviation Battalion	600
—Two Aviation Companies (Utility)	
—Aviation Company (Test and Evaluation)	
—Aviation Maintenance Company	
Total	2,070

SOURCES: RAND, based on data from Army TO&E, 1999, and the MFORCE database, 2001.

---

[12] DHS is at the time of this writing considering changes in its regional structure.

trol of the task force headquarters. In Army parlance, this force would be capable of handling most antiterrorism, counterterrorism, MACDIS, and other missions requiring support to law enforcement without augmentation from other Army forces. In extremely large incidents, the capability of each group could be increased by placing general-purpose forces under the temporary operational control of the group commander. This arrangement provides a process for increasing the capability of each group while ensuring that a law enforcement officer is present at all locations.

Training

This is a specialized unit that would require specific training to enable it to operate effectively within the constraints imposed by existing laws and regulations. The military police assigned to this organization would have a special skill identifier that would be used for assignment, promotion, and other personnel management actions. In addition, this unit would routinely conduct interagency exercises in support of DHS and the Justice Department.

Legal Issues

There is nothing in this response that would require modifications to federal or state statutes governing the use of the military within the United States. As a Title 10 force, this unit would be subject to the limitations imposed by the *Posse Comitatus* Act, other federal statutes, and relevant DoD directives. See Appendix B.

Command and Control

Because of their dedicated HLS mission, the combating terrorism task force would be a component of the U.S. Army Forces Command and assigned to the combatant command of NORTHCOM.

Give National Guard Primary Responsibility for HLS

A fourth HLS possibility is that terrorist attacks and other large-scale domestic emergencies would overwhelm the capabilities of civilian organizations and the National Guard and active Army forces would be unable to fill the gap, because the nation's priorities have called for them to be deployed in significant numbers overseas. Major deployments of Army active forces along with combat and combat support units overseas in Bosnia, Kosovo, Afghanistan, and Iraq have left fewer and fewer of these soldiers in the United States available to respond to domestic emergencies.

An Army response could be to give the National Guard, in its historical role under the state governors, primary responsibility for HLS activities, both those that are long term, such as critical infrastructure protection, and those involving quick or large-scale responses. The rapid-response capability would be achieved through the creation of a new civil support battalion (CSB) in ten multistate regions.[13] It would provide the heart of the National Guard capability for HLS with specialized training, capable of drawing on other National Guard units as necessary.

This Army response would not raise the end strength for the National Guard. Instead, it would carve out nearly 9,000 billets from the existing Guard force to make the new units. Nor would it increase the caps on Active Guard Reserves[14] or National Guard technicians.[15] Manpower would be reassigned within that pool.

The CSBs would be fully capable of replacing the two brigades assigned the Military Assistance for Civil Disturbances (Garden Plot) mission as well as the QRF and RRF units in the active Army and National Guard for HLS missions. Other active Army units and

---

[13] The CSBs in this response would be dispersed geographically within whatever regional DHS structure emerges.

[14] The Active Guard and Reserve (AGR) comprises personnel on voluntary active duty providing full-time support to National Guard, Reserve, and active component organizations for the purpose of organizing, administering, recruiting, instructing, or training the Reserve components. National Guard AGR personnel are managed by the states in peacetime and receive the same pay as active component soldiers. See DoD (1999).

[15] National Guard technicians are full-time personnel in "Excepted Federal Service." Technicians are civilians who are required to be part of the Selected Reserve in order to fill their positions and wear a National Guard uniform to work. Technicians can be moved to state active-duty status for Military Support to Civil Authorities (MSCA) operations (Stilley, 2003; Sarcione, 2003).

those in the National Guard and USAR would be able to focus on their warfighting missions.

Characteristics of Response

In this Army response, ten CSBs would be created. Each CSB would be ready to deploy in domestic emergencies within 18 hours of notification.[16] It would be able to carry out all the general HLS tasks, including communications, emergency medical care, search and rescue, engineering support, and emergency provision of food, water, and shelter. It would also have the ability to support local law enforcement by conducting general security operations. In the event of a large-scale incident that exceeds the CSB's capabilities, the CSBs would provide the command and control for augmentation by other National Guard forces from within the state, by CSBs from other regions, or by National Guard units from other states deployed consistent with regional and national compacts. By virtue of their training, the CSBs could work side by side and quickly integrate their capabilities with those of local first responders, state and federal agencies, and specialized counterterrorism and WMD units, such as the Marine Corps' CBIRF and National Guard WMD-CSTs.

Each battalion would have approximately 900 soldiers.[17] To provide a full-time planning cell and quick response capability, one-third of the CSB would be full-time positions, staffed by both AGRs in Title 32 status and civilian technicians working for the National Guard.[18] The remaining two-thirds would be part-time, drilling

---

[16] Notification occurs when a request for assistance has been made by a governor and approved by the Department of Defense. There will always be a lag time between when an incident occurs and the time a unit is notified. During this time it is anticipated that CSBs will begin initial preparation for recall in the event of notification.

[17] Because their missions would be somewhat different, the CSBs created in this response would be different from the domestic support battalions that would be created as part of the antiterrorism groups in the "Provide Rapid and Dedicated Combating Terrorism Force" response.

[18] For fiscal year 2003, Congress authorized a total of 50,264 AGR and technician positions—24,562 AGRs and 25,702 technicians. See Sarcione (2003) and Department of the Army (2003).

Guardsmen who agree to be on special ready status so that the governor could call them up within 12 hours. The CSB in each region would be tailored to meet the requirements of all states that are part of the region. The force of ten CSBs would total some 9,000 soldiers.

Paying for these CSBs would be done as today for the National Guard. The federal government would use Title 32 funds for manning, equipping, and training. The costs associated with HLS operations could be paid for by the requesting state, Title 32 funds (with statutory changes), or Title 10 funds if the unit were federalized.

The force structure in this response would be derived from an existing National Guard organization, the Forward Support Battalion, augmented with a communications platoon as well as military police, engineer, and transportation companies (see Table 3.4).

The CSB's headquarters detachment would be designed to control other National Guard units from the affected state or region and to accommodate an Air National Guard planning and liaison cell to enhance the CSB with Air National Guard aviation, aeromedical, engineering, and other capabilities. Designated platoons (approximately 40 soldiers each) in each CSB will be "ready" for rapid deployment. Full-time Guardsmen in ready platoons would be on a four-hour return-to-base order. Part-time soldiers would have to report

Table 3.4
Illustrative CSB Force Structure

Unit Type		Strength
Headquarters detachment		51
Communications platoon*		25
Supply company		62
Maintenance company		167
Medical company		100
Military police company*		177
Transportation company		167
Engineer company*		145
	Total	894

SOURCES: RAND, based on data from Army TO&E, 1999, and the MFORCE database, 2001.
NOTE: * indicates units added to a typical forward support battalion structure specifically to support the HLS mission.

to their units within 12 hours of recall. With a unit fully mustered in 12 hours, it should be ready to be deployed within 18 hours of notification. During exigent circumstances, this time could be reduced.

A CSB could be manned by using volunteers from National Guard units located within each region or recruited nationally, if necessary.[19] Table 3.5 lists the National Guard's Force Structure Allowance (FSA) (its authorized and funded positions) in each of today's Federal Emergency Management Agency (FEMA) regions and indicates that, in principle, manning an 894-person CSB would not be that difficult.

Training

All CSB personnel would need to be familiar with the incident command systems used by the states in their region and be trained for operations in a CBRN-contaminated environment. For HLS tasks, transportation, communications, and supply personnel will require minimal training above that necessary to be proficient in a Military

Table 3.5
Army National Guard Force Structure Allowance by FEMA Region for Fiscal Year 2003

Region	FSA
FEMA Region I	22,860
FEMA Region II	20,611
FEMA Region III	40,406
FEMA Region IV	84,243
FEMA Region V	57,809
FEMA Region VI	47,993
FEMA Region VII	25,845
FEMA Region VIII	20,131
FEMA Region IX	29,224
FEMA Region X	18,071
Total	367,193

SOURCE: National Guard Bureau (undated).

---

[19] The National Guard Bureau has implemented a nationwide recruitment strategy to staff the Army's Ground-Based Midcourse Defense brigade. This brigade will serve as a component of the future Ballistic Missile Defense System, and it will be manned almost entirely by National Guard personnel (Thie et al., 2003, p. 12).

Occupational Specialty (MOS), while engineers, medical personnel, and military police are likely to require more extensive training because these specialties must be familiar with the emergency response protocols used in the states within their respective region. Additionally, states may require additional training and certifications beyond the training required for MOS qualification for these specialties.

Legal Issues

This response would require the same statutory changes as in our first Army response: authorizing the use of Title 32 funds for HLS "training and activities," permitting Guardsman when operating in other states to carry out law enforcement missions, and providing Guardsmen with federal tort protections. It would also require that all the states in a region and those neighboring be signatories of an EMAC.

Command and Control

The CSB elements will be under the command of the adjutant general in the state where they are based. When an incident occurs that requires the deployment of the CSB, operational control of the CSB will be given to the adjutant general of the receiving state. To provide for such a contingency, each State Joint Force Headquarters (SJFHQ) must be capable of assuming operational control of a brigade-size or larger force.[20] The Commander of NORTHCOM will command the CSBs if they are moved to federal, Title 10 status.

---

[20] As of October 1, 2003, the State Area Commands (STARCs) will be disbanded and replaced by an SJFHQ. These organizations will be staffed by members of the Army and Air National Guard and their role will be to plan and conduct operations within the state. The SJFHQ will be a nondeployable organization. The adjutant generals of each state will command the organization. This headquarters could be placed in Title 10 status to allow it to command federal forces operating within the state, while maintaining the remainder of the National Guard in the state on state active duty as required.

Create Dedicated USAR Support Pool for HLS

A fifth HLS possibility is that terrorist attacks and other domestic emergencies will require quick and specialized responses, beyond the capabilities of civilian organizations and the state National Guard militia, that the Army cannot adequately provide, given that critical support units in the USAR are deployed overseas, require time to mobilize, or are subject to statutory constraints on their use within the United States.

Many of the types of support units particularly needed in past Army disaster relief operations are located primarily in the USAR and will likely remain so, even given the Army's plans for augmenting support units in the active force.[21] DoD policy is to give reservists 30 days' notification before being mobilized to provide them time to take care of their personal affairs, although in past emergencies this policy has been disregarded.[22] Steps are under way in the USAR to create an "alert" USAR force package for rapid deployment of these support units, but these units are also available for overseas contingencies.[23] Finally, current federal law generally forbids the mobilization of the USAR for missions within the United States, except in response to declared national emergencies, WMD attacks, or terrorist events or threats with the potential for significant loss of life or property.[24]

---

[21] See discussion of Army reorganization plans in Roosevelt (2004).

[22] See Chu (2002). Thomas F. Hall (2002), Assistant Secretary of Defense for Reserve Affairs, stated that, while DoD policy is to give reserve personnel 30 days' notification, in times of crisis, that requirement would be waived.

[23] For general description of USAR reorganization plans, see Hess (2004).

[24] See 10 USCA §§ 12301, 12304 (2003). In particular, 10 USCA § 12304 provides, in pertinent part:

  (b)   The [mobilization] authority under subsection (a) includes authority to order a [Selected Reserve] unit . . . to active duty to provide assistance in responding to an emergency involving – (1) a use or threatened use of a weapon of mass destruction; or (2) a terrorist attack or threatened terrorist attack in the United States that results, or could result, in catastrophic loss of life or property.

An Army response would be to dedicate a pool of USAR support units to an exclusive HLS mission, to give them specialized training, to make them available for contingencies in a timelier manner, and to remove the statutory restrictions on their use in domestic emergencies.

Although this USAR force pool could perform a variety of HLS missions, it is not intended by itself to fulfill all potential demands—e.g., airport security—and in these events would be supplemented with other Army resources. This response does not assume an increase in the end strength cap for the USAR, so the USAR support pool would draw on existing reserve units. The USAR support pool would replace the current post–September 11 RRFs and QRFs in the active Army.

While this response would entail a reduction in USAR support units available for overseas deployment, it could nevertheless offer a serendipitous benefit to the active Army by reducing HLS demands for active units in the event of rapid, large-scale HLS contingencies.

Characteristics of Response

This Army response would dedicate a pool of 7,560 soldiers in USAR support units: transportation, signal, civil affairs, military police, quartermaster, and chemical (reconnaissance). The types of units chosen are those most often called for to carry out HLS tasks, and are noteworthy also for being historically underrepresented in the active army and disproportionately concentrated in the USAR and the Army National Guard (See Table 3.6).

The USAR force pool would be located in different parts of the United States in order to facilitate responding to HLS contingencies anywhere in the country. Although the Reservists would not be on active duty, they would be notified of their priority HLS status, and would be on call for a more rapid activation (e.g., less than seven

---

(c) No unit or member of a reserve component may be ordered to active duty under this section . . . except as provided in subsection (b), to provide assistance to either the Federal Government or a State in time of a serious natural or manmade disaster, accident or catastrophe.

days). See Table 3.7 for the types of units that form the USAR support pool.

Training

The dedicated HLS support units in the USAR would receive specialized training for a full portfolio of HLS tasks. Their training would be carried out with Title 10 funds, as is the case today.

Table 3.6
Illustrative USAR and Army National Guard Contributions to the Army for Selected Support Units

Unit Type	USAR Units	Army National Guard Units	Combined % Total Army
Chemical Battalions	8	1	75
Chemical Brigades	3	0	100
Transportation Composite Groups	4	1	80
Motor Battalions	12	2	78
Military Police Battalions	19	12	66
Military Police Brigades	2	2	43
Civil Affairs Units	36	0	97
Signal Battalions	5	26	36
Signal Brigades	1	3	20

SOURCE: Abstracted from OSD (2001).
NOTE: These numbers are likely to shift somewhat in coming years as a result of Army plans to increase the Army's support forces in key specialties, including military police, transportation, and civil affairs units (Roosevelt, 2004).

Table 3.7
Illustrative USAR Support Unit Pool

Unit Type	Strength
Military Police Companies (12)	2,160
Signal Battalions (2)	1,200
Civil Affairs Battalions (4)	880
Transportation Companies (8)	2,000
Quartermaster Companies (4)	800
Chemical Companies (4)	520
Total	7,560

SOURCES: RAND, based on data from the Army TO&E, 1999, and the MFORCE database, 2001.

Legal Issues

Current statutory authority does not impose specific time limitations on mobilization for the USAR. Nevertheless, current DoD policy would need to be revised to fully realize the benefits of the proposed USAR force pool (10 USCA § 12301[e] [2003]). Statutory relief would also be required to give the USAR the flexibility to carry out all HLS missions, such as disaster relief, not related to terrorism.

Command and Control

The USAR force pool would be apportioned to NORTHCOM for HLS mission planning and would not be included in the planning of other combatant commanders for wartime use. In the event of an HLS mobilization, the USAR force pool would serve under the command authority of NORTHCOM.

Summary

The five Army responses are designed to improve the Army's ability to meet the different HLS possibilities. For a summary of these benefits and for the ways the responses were accomplished, see Figure 3.1.

Figure 3.1
HLS Benefits of Army Responses

Response	Benefits				How Accomplished	
	HLS units are...			AC Overseas Readiness	Force Structure	Planning
	More responsive	Available	Specially trained			
Army National Guard Training			X			
AC/Army National Guard HLS Ready Brigade	X	X	X			
AC/Combating Terrorism Force	X	X	X			
Army National Guard Primary HLS Responsibility	X	X	X	X		
Dedicate Rapid USAR Units	X	X	X	X		

RAND *MG221-3.1*

CHAPTER FOUR

The Price of the Army Responses

While the potential Army responses to the HLS possibilities developed in the previous chapter would improve the Army's capabilities for HLS, they are not without costs—financial and otherwise. So before the Army can decide whether to take steps to hedge against the risks that it could find itself unprepared for in these ways, it is important to examine what price it must pay. This chapter evaluates the potential costs of the Army responses defined in Chapter Three, including the costs of raising or not raising the Army's manpower caps, the costs to the Army's other missions, the rough financial costs, and the costs in the form of provoking political resistance.

Manpower Caps: Opportunity Costs or Increased Financial Costs

By design, the Army responses developed in Chapter Three do not involve an increase in any of the congressionally mandated caps on Army personnel in the active component, USAR, National Guard, the AGR, or Army technicians. So the active and National Guard forces created for HLS in the "Provide Rapid and Dedicated Combating Terrorism Force" response and the "Give National Guard Primary Responsibility for HLS" response would come at the expense of other Army capabilities. The Army would, however, have the flexibility to draw them from any other parts of the same component.

These opportunity costs could be removed by raising the relevant cap, but this would incur two other costs: a financial penalty for increasing the Army's force structure and for annual operating costs and potentially a political cost for raising the caps and increasing the Army budget.

If in the "Provide Rapid and Dedicated Combating Terrorism Force" response the Army created an entirely new task force of 6,200 active-duty soldiers to provide support to law enforcement for HLS, the startup cost would be roughly $3.2 billion and the annual operating cost would be roughly $400 million, based on the cost of establishing, training, and operating two-fifths of a division of light forces. That estimate is rough and assumes that the costs of standing up a new light division of 15,000 soldiers would be roughly $8 billion and the cost to operate and man that division would be roughly $1 billion each year.[1]

If in the "Give National Guard Primary Responsibility for HLS" response the Army added the 3,000 full-time Guardsmen to the National Guard to staff the headquarters and ready elements of the CSBs (nearly 300 per battalion), the annual operating cost for the full-time AGR force would be roughly $235 million. This estimate assumes the cost per AGR is, on average, $80,000 per year. It does not include any costs for conversion of the units (startup costs), which are likely to be small.

Costs to the Army's Overseas Missions

All but the first Army response would have an impact on the Army's ability to conduct its missions overseas because each would dedicate forces for HLS. In the "Create a Dedicated Rapid-Reaction Brigade" response, an Army combat brigade and its division slice would be unavailable. This cost to overseas missions would be shared equally between the active component and the National Guard. The "Pro-

---

[1] This estimate is derived from CBO (2003).

vide Rapid and Dedicated Combating Terrorism Force" response would require the Army to reduce the size of the active component force that would be available for overseas missions by roughly two brigades. Some 9,000 Guardsmen in the CSBs would not be available for overseas missions in the "Give National Guard Primary Responsibility for HLS" response. In the "Create Dedicated USAR Support Pool for HLS" response, about 7,500 USAR soldiers would not be deployable overseas.

Financial Costs

All of the potential Army responses involve financial costs. (See Table 4.1 for rough estimates.) Note that these estimates are intended to capture the approximate magnitude rather than the precise cost.

The first two responses would require increases in annual spending to operate and train the forces. The next two would entail some one-time startup costs to convert units from one type to another. If the Army's budget remained unchanged, other programs or operations would have to be cut to pay for increasing HLS readiness.

The "Improve National Guard HLS Capabilities" response would increase Title 32 funding to pay for HLS training and pre-planned activities of certain National Guard units and personnel. This funding would be additive to preserve the readiness of National Guard units for its other missions. Assuming that 10 percent of the Guardsmen in every state would receive two days of HLS training each year, the annual cost of this response would be $20 million. That cost assumes that the compensation cost for each four-hour training unit (known as a Unit Training Assembly) would average $100 per Guardsman, according to National Guard Bureau cost models. This estimate is based on a National Guard end strength of 350,000 and assumes that Guardsmen would receive four training units in two days, as they do today. It also includes roughly 50 percent more funding to cover the noncompensation related costs of exercises and training.

The "Create a Dedicated Rapid-Reaction Brigade" response would have to cover the cost of using National Guard units as part of the rotation for a dedicated HLS ready brigade. If National Guard forces provided half of the units each year, the Army would have to increase operations and support costs by roughly $200 million a year. If the National Guard were to provide forces for three-quarters of the year, as has happened at times with rotations in Bosnia, annual costs for this response would rise to roughly $400 million. Those estimates assume that the operations and support cost for each soldier is, on average, $80,000 per year and that 3,600 Guardsmen would be activated for four months twice a year—including three months on ready status and a total of one month to get ready and stand down.[2]

The "Provide Rapid and Dedicated Combating Terrorism Force" response would incur startup costs for converting active forces to the specialized units required for the rapidly deployable anti-terrorism and counterterrorism force. These costs could range from $1 billion to $1.4 billion. This estimate includes the costs to build the infrastructure for the forces and to purchase their equipment.[3]

Because the "Give National Guard Primary Responsibility for HLS" response shifts Guardsmen from their current duties to those of the CSBs, the Title 32 funding for personnel and training would not change. The costs of standing up the civil support battalions and converting existing units would range from roughly $400 million to $600 million.

The "Create Dedicated USAR Support Pool for HLS" response to HLS missions would probably not involve much cost because the necessary personnel and equipment exist in the USAR today.

---

[2] The operations and support cost is based on CBO (2003).

[3] The infrastructure costs for this estimate and the estimates for the "Give National Guard Primary Responsibility for HLS" response are based on the costs of consolidating a brigade in Germany as described in 5th Signal Command (undated). The range in the estimates reflects the difference between using existing barracks and having to build new ones. The estimates for the equipment costs for these two responses are from Army Cost Analysis Center, *FORCES Model*, 2003. These estimates do not include the costs to train the forces for their new missions.

Table 4.1
Estimated Costs of Illustrative Army Responses
($ Millions)

Army Response	Startup Costs	Annual Costs
Army National Guard Training	0	20
AC/Army National Guard HLS Ready Brigade	0	200
AC Combating Terrorism Force	1,000 to 1,400	0
Army National Guard Primary HLS Responsibility	400 to 600	0
Dedicate Rapid USAR Units	0	0

NOTE: Assumes no changes in Army end strength.

Political Resistance Costs

The Army responses can also be expected to provoke different types of political opposition. Resistance throughout the government is likely, whether change involves new statutes or past Army practices. Note that the Department of Defense has not supported a bill (S.215, GUARD Act of 2003) proposed by Senator Dianne Feinstein (D-Calif.) in 2003 and cosponsored by many others in the Senate, that would explicitly permit the National Guard to spend Title 32 funds for HLS training, as in the "Improve National Guard HLS Capabilities" response.

The Department of Defense has also expressed opposition to dedicating any additional military forces to HLS, largely because it could reduce the flexibility of U.S. forces for warfighting and other overseas contingencies. The Department of Defense has been clear in saying that the National Guard's WMD-CSTs and the Emergency Preparedness Liaison Officers in each state are the only dedicated forces needed (DoD, 2002, p. 38). Indeed, even the wisdom of maintaining the WMD-CSTs as a dedicated HLS force is questioned by the senior leadership of the National Guard Bureau, who argue, instead, that they should be organized and equipped for overseas deployments while maintaining a unique capability for operating within the United States (Blum, 2003). Although the Army today has specialized forces for supporting law enforcement agencies, developing a dedicated, active-duty force specifically for this purpose, as in the "Provide Rapid and Dedicated Combating Terrorism Force" response, is likely to face widespread resistance on Capitol Hill and also in the Army. Opposition could also arise to adding to the burden on the National Guard, by calling up a National Guard brigade as in the "Create a Dedicated Rapid-Reaction Brigade" response.

CHAPTER FIVE

Conclusions

The Army has played a critical role historically in ensuring the nation's security at home and can expect to be called on in the future to counter whatever enemy or terrorist threats arise and to respond to other types of domestic emergencies. In states across the country, the National Guard today is available to respond, just as it did in the case of the September 11 terrorist attacks. The Army stands ready for HLS missions with rapid-reaction forces in all of its components, although these forces are also on call for overseas contingencies. The Army has taken a number of steps to improve its planning and capabilities for HLS operations.

What this report has sought to do is to explore whether the Army should do more to hedge against the risk of being inadequately prepared, given a world where terrorists have demonstrated the willingness and capability to conduct mass-casualty attacks within the United States and where the capabilities of civilian law enforcement agencies and emergency responders are expanding but still untested.

To do this, we have designed a hybrid approach for dealing with HLS uncertainties and the Army's requirements—one that focuses on possibilities against which the Army might wish to hedge. These possibilities could arise for a variety of reasons: the Army lacks the specific training needed for HLS tasks, its forces are unable to deploy rapidly enough, or forces are not available because of competing demands. Our approach then defines ways in which the Army could prepare *today,* by conducting more specialized training, by improving its responsiveness, and/or by augmenting certain types of its capabilities.

Obviously, the Army would take such steps if they were cost-free. This is not the case, however. They would either require an increase in annual costs to operate and train the forces or entail one-time startup costs to convert units from one type to another. Unless the current manpower caps are raised, any new or dedicated HLS units would come at the expense of other Army capabilities and make them unavailable for overseas deployments, just at the time when demands for such deployments are increasing. There is the alternative of adding force structure, but the manning, equipping, and operating costs of such responses would add billions of dollars to the Army's budget.

What emerges from our analysis is that adopting any steps to improve the Army's HLS capabilities would result in *certain* costs today with only the *promise of benefits* in the future, were any of these HLS possibilities actually to arise. Without being able to predict the future, the choice for the nation then is what kinds of HLS risks it is willing to assume and whether to undertake a hedging strategy.

Based on our analysis, a multifaceted hedging strategy on the part of the Army could make sense.

First, given the National Guard's responsibility and availability to respond to domestic emergencies, the Army should support legislation that would make it possible for DoD to fund National Guard HLS activities and for the National Guard to share its resources more easily across state borders.

One way this could be accomplished is described in our "Improve National Guard HLS Capabilities" response and would in essence make it possible for the National Guard to conduct HLS training and activities as it does for counterdrug operations. The effectiveness of this step as a hedge would then depend on the amount of money the Army would make available during its annual budget process, which would in turn depend on other Army and DoD priorities. The Army should also seek the necessary statutory changes so that the USAR can conduct all HLS missions, including responses to natural disasters. These steps would have the effect of removing existing statutory constraints on the use of the Reserve for the full range of potential HLS activities.

Given the shortage of support units in the AC, the Army's current plans for rebalancing its active and reserve forces represent an important step, for they will improve the Army's ability to respond quickly, and with more appropriate capabilities, to large-scale domestic emergencies. The effectiveness of this hedge, however, for HLS would depend on whether these rebalanced AC resources are actually available for homeland security, not deployed overseas when they are needed in the United States.

So, second, given the possibility of their being unavailable and given the need, already acknowledged by DoD, for units in all of the Army's components to be ready and on alert for HLS emergencies, the Army should take the additional step of dedicating some forces to such emergencies, making them ready for rapid deployment and ensuring that they are appropriately trained.

This could be accomplished in different ways. One would be our "Create a Dedicated Rapid-Reaction Brigade," which would rotate between the AC and the National Guard, as in the Balkan peacekeeping operations. Another is our "Give National Guard Primary Responsibility for HLS" response that establishes regional civil support battalions in the National Guard. Our "Create Dedicated USAR Support Pool for HLS" response dedicates certain types of support forces in the USAR. Each of these responses involves units with the capabilities generally needed for managing the consequences of domestic emergencies.

The question arises, though, about whether the dedicated and ready forces in the Army hedging strategy should instead be composed of more-specialized units capable of supporting civilians in law enforcement activities, as in our "Provide Rapid and Dedicated Combating Terrorism Force" response.

Third, because the prospective capabilities and deficiencies of civilian organizations are so uncertain, the Army should hedge again by dedicating a mix of forces for HLS with some units trained in specialized law enforcement capabilities.

The problem, of course, is that the HLS benefits of these dedicated Army forces come at the expense of the Army's flexibility to deploy these forces overseas. So a decision will be needed in the Army's hedging strategy about where these forces should come from—the active Army, the National Guard, and/or the USAR? This in turn requires an assessment of the relative costs. This is especially difficult today because the cost to the nation of forgoing overseas deployments in any of these components is very uncertain and could be high. One way would be to draw these units equally across the three components. However, the active Army provides the most flexible and available forces for overseas deployments, and its effectiveness will continue to depend on having supporting USAR units.

So, fourth, the dedicated units should be drawn from the National Guard, not only for these reasons but also because of its historical experiences in domestic emergencies, links to state and local emergency responders, and relatively low cost compared to full-time active-duty forces. To be effective as a hedge, the National Guard would need to create standing regional homeland task forces across the country, along the lines of our "Give National Guard Primary Responsibility for HLS" response, with units dedicated and trained for homeland security, and with capabilities for rapid response.

In the end, what is needed is for the nation to decide that it is worth bearing the costs today associated with the Army becoming better prepared for HLS than it presently is (in the aftermath of September 11) to *hedge* against a future that is uncertain, but one that could involve serious risks if the Army were found unprepared.

The Army's Capabilities for Homeland Security

The Army is composed of three primary forces, also known as components: the active component (AC), the U.S. Army Reserve (USAR), and the Army National Guard. The mix of active and reserve forces is designed to support the "Total Force" doctrine: the notion that any major mobilization of the Army for war should require forces from both the AC and the reserve component (RC).[1] The Total Force doctrine emerged from the post-Vietnam era, and reflected the conviction that a required commitment of RC forces to fighting a war would help ensure political support with regard to future Army operations. Partly as a consequence of this doctrine, the AC/RC force structure has evolved to concentrate many of the Army's combat support and combat service support personnel and functions within the USAR, while the AC has retained a high proportion of combat and combat support units.[2] Mobilization and deployment of the Army for large-scale sustained combat operations requires a large number of support and service support personnel, and, consequently, the Army cannot fight wars without drawing heavily on resources from the RC. This will still be the case, even after the Army's current restructuring initiatives. As an unintended result, operations tempo for some RC support units has been very high in recent years.[3]

---

[1] See discussion in Owens (2001).

[2] See, e.g., CBO (1997, p. xiv).

[3] See, e.g., GAO (2003, pp. 10–13).

As currently configured, the AC and RC are roughly equal in terms of end strength, with approximately 500,000 soldiers in each.[4] The RC is further divided into two separate and distinct forces, the U.S. Army Reserve (USAR) with 206,000 soldiers and the Army National Guard with 352,000. While both elements are responsible for augmenting the AC, organizational and legal differences have a profound affect on the current utilization of each. For example, the USAR is composed almost exclusively of combat support (CS),[5] combat service support (CSS) units,[6] and Mobilization Base Expansion units (MBEs)[7] with a very limited number of combat units.[8] Conversely, the Army National Guard is composed primarily of combat forces, with a more limited number of CS and CSS units.[9] See Figure A.1 for the makeup of each of the Army components.

While both parts of the RC are responsible for augmenting the active component in times of war, they have different historical roots and different legal authorities. USAR is a federal reserve force that provides CS and CSS capabilities to augment active Army resources, which have been used largely overseas. It consists primarily of part-

---

[4] The composition of the Total Force is as follows: 46 percent active, 20 percent Reserve, and 34 percent National Guard. The end strength of the total Army is 1,040,000 with approximately 482,000 in the AC and 558,000 in the RC.

[5] The CS units include signal, chemical, military police, engineer, military intelligence, psychological operations, and medium helicopter support.

[6] The CSS units include medical, finance, supply, quartermaster, transportation, judge advocate, petroleum/water, logistics, administrative services, civil affairs, and fixed-wing aviation.

[7] The MBE units include training divisions, garrison, school, hospital, depot support, and port operation.

[8] The composition of the USAR is as follows: 54 percent CSS, 18 percent CS, 27 percent MBEs, and 1 percent combat units. See "About the Army Reserve a Federal Force," available at http://www.army.mil/usar.

[9] The combat forces include 15 enhanced Separate Brigades, eight divisions, three strategic brigades (31st SAB, 92nd SIB, and 207th Scout Group), and two Special Forces groups (19th and 20th). These forces constitute 52 percent of the Army National Guard. The rest of the Guard is broken down as follows: 22 percent CSS, 17 percent CS, and 9 percent non-deployable state headquarters. See U.S. Army National Guard (2004); Fleming (2001).

Figure A.1
Makeup of Each Army Component

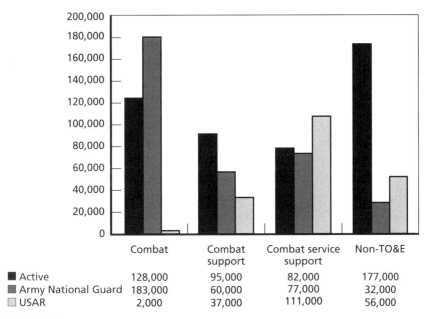

	Combat	Combat support	Combat service support	Non-TO&E
■ Active	128,000	95,000	82,000	177,000
▨ Army National Guard	183,000	60,000	77,000	32,000
☐ USAR	2,000	37,000	111,000	56,000

RAND *MG221-A.1*

time volunteers that can be called into federal service to support Army missions and is essential for any large-scale deployment of the Army. USAR receives all of its funding through Title 10 sources and is governed by the same statutes as the active component. As discussed in Appendix B, current statutes and regulations limit the employment of the USAR in HLS tasks except under exigent circumstances.

The National Guard is unique within DoD because it has dual state and federal missions. Until called into federal service, the Guard is a state entity that can be used by the individual governors in any manner consistent with state law, provided federal funds are not used for these state activities. While the National Guard has struggled to balance these roles, the state mission has traditionally been secondary to the federal, primarily because the lion's share of the National Guard's funding for training, operations, and equipment comes from the federal government through Title 32 of the U.S. Code. The National Guard's primary federal mission is to provide a combat reserve for active forces. Consequently, it is focused, trained, and equipped for missions that until recently have been largely overseas. Secondarily, with its large number of combat forces, all located within the United States, the Army National Guard has always been envisioned as the primary ground force to be employed in the event it became necessary to militarily defend the nation against a foreign aggressor. As a state force, the National Guard's peacetime domestic role is "to provide units organized, equipped, and trained to function effectively in protection of life and property and the preservation of peace, order, and public safety under competent orders of state authorities, or federal officials if federalized" (Baca, 1995).

As a result of its dual state and federal status, the National Guard also has a unique command structure. Unlike the active component and USAR, which always remains under the command of a unified military commander and, by extension, the Secretary of Defense and the President, National Guardsmen are under the command of the individual state adjutant general and the respective Governor unless called to federal service. Consequently, certain laws, such as the *Posse Comitatus* Act,[10] do not apply to National Guardsmen when they are performing their state missions. Conversely, other laws, such as the Anti-Deficiency Act, limit activities that a National Guard commander can undertake (see Appendix B) unless funded by the state.[11]

The AC/RC mix has direct implications for the Army's role in carrying out HLS activities. First, past RAND research on Army

---

[10] 18 USC Section 1385.

[11] The Anti-Deficiency Act (31 USC, Section 1341) prohibits the expenditure or obligation of federal funds for any purpose other than those for which Congress has specifically authorized and appropriated. Except as otherwise specifically authorized by Congress, the Anti-Deficiency Act precludes the use of federal funds for any purpose other than preparing the National Guard to perform its federal mission. This Act prevents National Guard units from conducting HLS training using Title 32 funds. In California, Arizona, and Washington, for example, HLS training is paid for by state funds. If the emergency is large enough to warrant federal assistance, reimbursement for this training is requested.

operations in domestic disaster relief has suggested that Army support personnel, currently units that are in abundance within the USAR, may be particularly useful for these types of operations in the future.[12] To the extent that RC support personnel are also in great demand for overseas deployments and protecting Army installations within the United States, those personnel will be correspondingly less available for use in domestic HLS operations. Note that the AC is particularly well suited for rapid responses to large-scale HLS operations and has been used in that capacity in a number of historical operations. When a U.S. disaster threatens to overwhelm the capabilities of local civilians and state National Guard units, then AC forces are likely to be called on for additional assistance. It has yet to be seen the degree to which the recent enactment of the Emergency Mutual Assistance Compact (EMAC) will reduce the reliance on the active component for future large-scale disasters. Despite the AC's core capacity for undertaking rapid, large-scale responses, it is nevertheless relatively underresourced in a number of categories of support units likely to be of central importance for large HLS emergencies.[13] This is especially true today when the size of the active component is 62 percent of what it was in 1990, and the majority of those forces are engaged abroad. In sum, AC/RC force structure has both direct and collateral effects on the Army's ability to execute HLS missions.

---

[12] For discussion of projected support unit requirements in civil support, disaster relief, and HLS missions, see Pirnie and Francisco (1998).

[13] For a general discussion of the allocation of specialized types of Army units across the AC and RC, see OSD (2001, pp. 2–4).

Legal Issues for the Army in Homeland Security

Using any of the Army's components for HLS can raise important legal and policy issues. It is clear that Article IV of the Constitution mandates that the federal government protect the states from foreign invasion and, when duly requested by the state, domestic violence.[1] When the federal military is employed for these purposes, command authority governing the conduct of the operations resides squarely with the President. Not only does the President have the authority to employ the military in these circumstances, but he also has the constitutional responsibility. However, the critical issue is when can the President employ the federal military outside of the situations contemplated by Article IV, Section 4—that is, outside of an invasion or the state having requested assistance to quell domestic violence?

The *Posse Comitatus* Act[2]

Using the military within the borders of the United States raises concerns, and consequently a number of laws have been passed to limit

---

[1] Article IV, Section 4 of the U.S. Constitution states: "The United States shall guarantee to every State in this Union a Republican Form of Government, and shall protect each of them against Invasion; and on application of the Legislature, or of the Executive *[of the states]* (when the Legislature cannot be convened) against domestic Violence."

[2] For a detailed discussion of the *Posse Comitatus* Act, see Demaine and Rosen (forthcoming); Advisory Panel to Assess Domestic Response Capabilities for Terrorism Involving Weapons of Mass Destruction (2000, p. 3, Appendix R); and Kellman (2002).

and proscribe such use. The most commonly cited limitation on the use of the military is the *Posse Comitatus* Act, a law passed in 1878 that, in the wake of the disputed 1876 presidential election, would end the use of federal troops to enforce voting laws within formerly Confederate states. As is now widely known, this Act prohibits the use of the military to enforce civil criminal law within the United States, except as otherwise authorized by the Constitution or statute.[3]

As has been noted in recent studies,[4] however, there are numerous exceptions to this law relating to counterdrug operations,[5] certain acts of terrorism involving the use of specified WMD,[6] and the protection of such designated individuals as the President, Vice President, and certain members of Congress and foreign dignitaries.[7] Perhaps the broadest exception, however, is the power given to the President by Article IV of the Constitution and subsequent legislation, which states that the President may "call into Federal Service such of the militia of the other States, and use such of the armed forces, *as he considers necessary* to enforce the laws and suppress the rebellion" (10 USC, Chapter 15, Section 232).[8] The important part to remember about the *Posse Comitatus* Act is that federal court rul-

---

[3] The *Posse Comitatus* Act, 18 USC, Section 1385, states, "Whoever, except in the cases and under circumstances expressly authorized by the Constitution or Act of Congress, willfully uses any part of the Army or the Air Force as a posse comitatus or otherwise to execute the laws shall be fined not more than $10,000 or imprisoned not more than two years, or both." Although the *Posse Comitatus* Act, by its own terms, applies to only the Army and the Air Force, the *Posse Comitatus* Act's restrictions have been extended to the Navy and Marine Corps as a matter of DoD policy through DoDD 5525.5.

[4] See Brennan (2002, pp. 37–42). For a more detailed discussion of laws governing the use of the military in HLS, see Advisory Panel to Assess Domestic Response Capabilities for Terrorism Involving Weapons of Mass Destruction (2000, Appendix R).

[5] Rather than being an exception to the *Posse Comitatus* Act, some have argued that the statute on counterdrug activities clarified the bounds of the *Posse Comitatus* Act,

[6] Exceptions are more broadly for any illegal use of chemical, biological, or nuclear weapons or their precursors.

[7] A note to 18 USC 3056, Presidential Protection Assistance Act of 1976 (PL 94-524) authorizes the military to help the Secret Service protect designated "protected persons."

[8] The totality and limitations of presidential authorities pursuant to Article IV are a matter of legal debate involving the presidency, legislature, and judiciary. This subject is addressed in more detail in Demaine and Rosen (forthcoming).

ings have stipulated that it only governs the federal military and the National Guard when serving in its federal capacity. Furthermore, the *Posse Comitatus* Act primarily establishes limitations on the use of the military in a direct civilian law enforcement, such as arrest, search, and seizure.[9] In exigent circumstances, however, many argue that the President has wide constitutional and statutory authorities to take those actions necessary to protect the United States, including employment of the military to enforce the law.[10]

The Stafford Act

While limitations have been placed on the military with regard to enforcement of civil criminal laws, statutes have also been written to specifically authorize the military to provide non–law enforcement support to the states and other federal agencies during times of emergency. The most comprehensive of these is the Robert T. Stafford Disaster Relief Act of 1984, which authorizes the President to employ federal military forces and capabilities after a natural or manmade disaster following a request by a state governor or legislature, and the declaration of a state of emergency by the President. Once an emergency is declared, federal forces can be used under the direction of the Federal Emergency Management Agency (FEMA).[11]

---

[9] The courts use three different tests to determine what activity constitutes the execution of the law and all of the tests potentially encompass far greater activity than just "arrest, search, and seizure." See, *United States v. Red Feather*, 392 F. Supp. 916 (D.S.D. 1975). DoDD 5525.5, *DoD Cooperation with Civilian Law Enforcement Officials*, provides other examples of prohibited actions.

[10] This is clearly the position taken by the Department of Defense. However, no court has ever discussed the issue. For a more detailed discussion of this subject, see Chapter Three of Demaine and Rosen (forthcoming).

[11] 42 USC, Section 5170, 5170b, and 5191, more commonly known as the Stafford Act. See also Executive Order 12673, dated March 23, 1989, DoDD 3025.1, and Army Regulation 500-60. This responsibility has recently been transferred to the Department of Homeland Security, of which FEMA is a part. See U.S. Congress, *Homeland Security Act of 2002*, Section 502. For more information on the Stafford Act and the preconditions it sets forth for the military to perform disaster relief tasks, see Winthrop (1997, pp. 3, 9–11).

Legal Status of the National Guard

The various federal laws governing the use of the military within the United States apply only to federal military forces. Members of the National Guard can be called to active duty in three ways. First, National Guard units and individuals, as part of the organized state militia, can be ordered to state active duty consistent with state constitutions and laws. It is under this status that the National Guard is most frequently employed to assist in dealing with forest fires, floods, hurricanes, critical infrastructure protection, and civil disturbances. While in this status, members of the National Guard are under the command and control of the state and receive funding from the state, although the state may later go to the federal government and seek reimbursement under the provisions of the Stafford Act.

As mentioned earlier, on the opposite end of the spectrum, National Guard units and members can be called to federal active duty under the provisions contained in Title 10 of U.S. Code, the same laws that govern active component forces. Title 10 also specifies that all members of the reserve component—including Army Reservists, individual reservists, and National Guardsmen—may be ordered to 15 days' involuntary active duty by the service secretaries or for up to 270 days by a presidential reserve call-up, two years by a partial mobilization called by the President, and for the duration of the war or other emergency plus six months by a full mobilization.[12] While in Title 10 status, the National Guard may also be called to active duty as a federal militia to repel an invasion, suppress an insurrection, or enforce the laws of the United States. While the orders for this type of mobilization are issued by the state governors, command and control is transferred to the federal government. While serving in this federal status, the activities of the Guard are governed by the same laws and regulations as the other components of the federal military, and command and control is exercised by the federal chain of command.

---

[12] 10 USC, Sections 12301, 12302, and 12304.

Between these two extremes lies Title 32 (National Guard) of the U.S. Code. While in a Title 32 status, the activities of the National Guard are funded by the federal government, but command and control remains with the state. The large majority of activations under the provisions of this statute, in terms of both number of activities and man-days, are for training purposes, which include weekend drill, annual training, and attendance at service schools. Members of the National Guard may also serve full time in the National Guard as a member of the Active Guard and Reserve (AGR) while in a Title 32 status. In the large majority of cases, Title 32 is used to assist in the training and readiness of National Guard members and units so they are prepared to fulfill their federal mission as a reserve combat force. In fact, Congress has passed legislation prohibiting the use of Title 32 funds for any purpose that does not directly relate to the federal mission of the National Guard. A dominant legal opinion within National Guard legal circles is that the so-called Anti-Deficiency Act precludes the use of federal "Title 32" dollars for any HLS activity because such activities are not designated as one of its federal missions.[13] This limitation could be changed simply by assigning National Guard units with an HLS mission when called to active duty.

DoD Policies Regulating the Use of Military Forces for HLS

DoD has a number of policies directing the military to assist civilian authorities in the event of a civil emergency, which is defined by DoD as "any natural or manmade disaster or emergency that causes or could cause substantial harm to the population, or infrastructure."[14] The nature of the emergency and the urgency of the action determines what level of DoD official is authorized to determine

---

[13] 31 USC, Section 1341, makes it a criminal offense for an officer or employee of the U.S. government to authorize an expenditure or obligation of funds exceeding the amount available in appropriations. Since HLS activities are not currently appropriated within Title 32, these funds cannot be used. An exception to this rule is the WMD-CSTs.

[14] DoDD 3025.12, Military Assistance for Civil Disturbances (MACDIS), paragraph E.2.1.5 (February 4, 1994).

whether to provide support and to determine the type and amount of assistance to be provided.

In certain circumstances, local military commanders may have to act to provide assistance in a nonmilitary setting without explicit statutory authority. DoD directives state that local military commanders and other DoD officials have "Immediate Response Authority" during civil disturbances and disaster relief to take action before a declaration of an emergency or major disaster if such assistance is requested by civil authorities and either the seriousness of the conditions or necessity for immediate action is warranted.[15]

DoD's support to civil authorities is generally referred to as Military Assistance to Civil Authorities (MACA). The most common way that DoD supports civilian authorities is under the provisions of the Stafford Act. In an effort to describe how and when such assistance will be provided, DoD published a policy on Military Support to Civil Authorities (MSCA).[16] While this policy is currently under review, it provides a statement of how it prepares for and responds to emergencies managed by FEMA through the Regional Military Emergency Coordinating teams. While the support that DoD provides may include actions undertaken pursuant to immediate response authority, it also addresses the employment of a wide range of DoD resources and establishes only three limitations: DoD personnel cannot provide assistance to law enforcement under this directive; civilian resources must be used before military resources, and such resources must have been determined to be insufficient to meet the demands of the emergency; and unless the Secretary of Defense

---

[15] A letter signed by the Deputy Secretary of Defense states that local commanders may "undertake immediate, unilateral, emergency response actions that involve measures to save lives, prevent human suffering, or mitigate great property damage, only when time does not permit the approval by higher headquarters." See Memorandum, Deputy Secretary of Defense to the Secretaries of the Military Departments, subject: DoD Year 2000 (Y2K) Support to Civil Authorities (February 22, 1999), available at www.army.mil/army-y2k/desecdef_dod_civil_support.htm. It should be noted, however, that no statutory exception to the *Posse Comitatus* Act exists for this purpose, and, consequently, legal questions concerning this directive have arisen as it relates to military personnel executing the law.

[16] DoDD 3025.1, Military Support to Civil Authorities (MSCA), January 15, 1993. Today, DoD uses the term Military Assistance to Civil Authorities (MACA) instead.

determines otherwise, the military's non-MSCA missions take priority.[17] DoD's response to Hurricane Andrew is a classic example of an emergency that required a large-scale DoD response consistent with this directive. Such operations require trained and ready personnel capable of providing such services as housing, food, and medical support during times of a disaster.

In addition to providing assistance in preparation for or in response to a disaster, MACA also encompasses those types of missions that relate to the employment of forces and capabilities to maintain law and order, protect property, and enhance security. The directive governing this type of activity states that any cooperation will "be consistent with the needs of national security and military preparedness, the historic tradition of limiting direct military involvement in civilian law enforcement activities, and the requirements of applicable law."[18] This is a wide category of responses that DoD provides to assist other federal agencies that includes DoD assistance for civil disturbance;[19] loans of equipment, facilities, or personnel to law enforcement agencies;[20] critical infrastructure protection; and domestic counterterrorism operations.[21] Any decision to employ federal military resources to respond to these types of domestic nonmilitary emergencies is made by the Secretary of Defense[22] after considering the following six criteria: *legality* (does the requested action

---

[17] DoDD 3025.1, A.2-6.

[18] DoDD 3025.15, Military Assistance to Civilian Authorities (MACA), February 18, 1997.

[19] DoDD 3025.12, Military Assistance for Civil Disturbances (MACDIS), February 18, 1997.

[20] DoDD 5525.5, DoD Cooperation with Civilian Law Enforcement Officials, December 20, 1997.

[21] A number of laws have been enacted to authorize direct military action to prevent or respond to incidents of catastrophic terrorism involving WMD, including nuclear, biological, and chemical weapons, which most notably are 10 USC Sections 175, 372, 380, 382, 12304, and 12310.

[22] The authority for MACA can be delegated no lower than a flag officer, general, or a civilian official confirmed by the U.S. Senate.

conform to federal law);[23] *lethality* (potential use of lethal force by or against the armed forces); *risk* (safety of DoD forces); *cost* (who pays and what is the impact on the DoD budget); *appropriateness* (whether conducting the mission is in DoD's interest); and *readiness* (impact on DoD's ability to perform its primary mission) (GAO, 2003, pp. 5–6). Recent examples of this type of operation include DoD assistance provided to the D.C. sniper case, counterdrug operations, and the military assistance provided to quell the Los Angeles riot. Any assistance provided under these conditions must comport with the *Posse Comitatus* Act.[24]

Interstate Compacts

Historically, most HLS activities are fulfilled through the use of the National Guard of the state affected. When these capabilities are insufficient, National Guard members from adjacent states may provide assistance through the provisions of multistate compacts, but only when such support is requested by the governor of the receiving state and approved by the governor of the supporting state. When this type of support is provided, all costs of the operation must be paid for by the receiving state. Until recently, compacts were ad hoc arrangements between adjacent states. In 1996, however, Congress authorized the establishment of a nationwide EMAC.[25] This agreement establishes a partnership between states that ratify the agreement to join forces to respond to emergencies ranging from toxic waste spills to hurricanes and acts of terrorism. The EMAC offers a quick and easy way for states to send equipment and personnel to

---

[23] In making this determination, DoD assesses statutory law, case law, and constitutional law.

[24] Enclosure 4 to DoDD 5525.5 includes a list of activities that may be undertaken that do not violate the *Posse Comitatus* Act, including actions to further a military or foreign affairs function of the United States, actions that are taken under the inherent right of the U.S. government to ensure the preservation of public order and to maintain government operations within its territory, the employment of military forces during an insurrection or domestic violence in a manner that hinders state execution of state or federal law, and any action taken with express statutory authority allowing direct military action to enforce civilian laws.

[25] Public Law 104-321.

assist in disaster relief in other states, provides a legally binding contractual arrangement that makes the requesting state responsible for all out-of-state costs of the operation, and makes the requesting state liable for the actions of out-of-state-personnel. As of August 2003, 49 states and two territories have either ratified the EMAC or are in the process of doing so. The only state that has demonstrated an unwillingness to adopt the EMAC is California.

As part of the state apparatus, the National Guard of signatory states are able to provide military assistance to other states in the event of any emergency or disaster when duly requested and approved.[26] While the existing EMAC is sufficient for disaster relief, it is not designed to enable National Guard members and units of one state to carry arms and enforce the laws or provide protection of another state. Currently, such actions would require that these units be federalized and placed under federal command and control. Further, unless National Guard personnel are in federal status, they do not enjoy the federal tort protections afforded to their counterparts in the Reserve or in the active component.

Even with a viable EMAC in place, certain disasters will require federal assistance. When this occurs, the employment of the federal military can be requested to augment the capabilities of federal civilian agencies. To determine the size and composition of the federal military response, a Defense Coordinating Officer coordinates with the Lead Federal Agency on the ground to determine the specific needs. As this assessment process is taking place, military units may be alerted to the potential mission to support civil authorities.

---

[26] Title 18 USC Section 1385.

Command Relationships

To effectively employ and husband the capabilities of military organizations, the Department of Defense has established policies with regard to the command and control of military units. These relationships are important because they provide a legal framework that governs the type and amount of authority that commanders may exercise. DoD describes four general types of command relationships: combatant command, coordinating authority, operational control, and tactical control. The most comprehensive of these is command, which is the power of the federal government vested in the President that is exercised in an unbroken chain from the President to the lowest grade soldier in the field by ensuring that all members of the military are under the combatant command of a unified or specified commander, such as Joint Forces Command, U.S. Northern Command (NORTHCOM), U.S. Space Command, or any other command listed in the Unified Command Plan.

This command authority, by law, can never be transferred. However, combatant commanders may, temporarily, place their assigned forces under the control of another entity when directed to do so by the Secretary of Defense or President. State governors have the same type of sovereign command authority over their militias: command authority is exercised by the governor through the state Adjutant General through the chain of command to the lowest soldier in the field.

Unlike command, which is a sovereign authority, operational control of forces can be transferred to organizations and entities outside the chain of command. For example, forces assigned to Joint Forces Command have been placed under the operational control of U.S. Central Command during the recent wars in Iraq and Afghanistan. Combatant command authority over these forces, however, remained with Joint Forces Command. Likewise, National Guardsmen from, say, New Jersey can be placed under the temporary operational control of the Adjutant General of New York when so directed by the Governor of New Jersey. In this situation, the command of the forces remains with the New Jersey National Guard, but the Governor of New York is permitted to direct their activities within his state so long as those orders are consistent with the agreement governing their employment.

Tactical control is more limiting than operational control and involves the detailed direction and control of movements or maneuvers within the operational area. It is also transferable.

Finally, coordinating authority is the authority given to one commander to coordinate the activities of disparate organizations. It does not represent a command relationship and is not directive in nature. U.S. NORTHCOM today exercises coordinating authority of all homeland defense and HLS activities of all federal forces and National Guard organizations within the United States. The commander has no authority to direct a particular unit to do anything unless or until such forces are placed under his operational control.

The following definitions are extracted verbatim from the *DoD Dictionary of Military Terms,* Joint Publication 1-02, as amended through June 5, 2003.

Combatant Command (Command Authority): Nontransferable command authority established by title 10 ("Armed Forces"), United States Code, section 164, exercised only by commanders of unified or specified combatant commands unless otherwise directed by the President or the Secretary of Defense. Combatant command (command authority) cannot be delegated and is the authority of a combatant commander to perform those functions of command over assigned forces involving organizing and employing commands and forces, assigning tasks, designating objectives, and giving authoritative direction over all aspects of military operations, joint training, and logistics necessary to accomplish the missions assigned to the command. Combatant command (command authority) should be exercised through the commanders of subordinate organizations. Normally this authority is exercised through subordinate joint force commanders and Service and/or functional component commanders. Combatant command (command authority) provides full authority to organize and employ commands and forces as the combatant commander considers necessary to accomplish assigned missions. Operational control is inherent in combatant command (command authority).

Coordinating Authority: A commander or individual assigned responsibility for coordinating specific functions or activities involving forces of two or more Military Departments, two or more joint force components, or two or more forces of the same Service. The commander or individual has the authority to require consultation between the agencies involved, but does not have the authority to compel agreement. In the event that essential agreement cannot be obtained, the matter shall be referred to the appointing authority. Coordinating authority is a consultation relationship, not an authority through which command may be exercised. Coordinating authority is more applicable to planning and similar activities than to operations.

Operational Control (OPCON): Command authority that may be exercised by commanders at any echelon at or below the level of combatant command. Operational control is inherent in combatant command (command authority) and may be delegated within the command. When forces are transferred between combatant commands, the command relationship the gaining commander will exercise (and the losing commander will relinquish) over these forces must be specified by the Secretary of Defense. Operational control is the authority to perform those functions of command over subordinate forces involving organizing and employing commands and forces, assigning tasks, designating objectives, and giving authoritative direction necessary to accomplish the mission. Operational control includes authoritative direction over all aspects of military operations and joint training necessary to accomplish missions assigned to the command. Operational control should be exercised through the commanders of subordinate organizations. Normally this authority is exercised through subordinate joint force commanders and Service and/or functional component commanders. Operational control normally provides full authority to organize commands and forces and to employ those forces as the commander in operational control considers necessary to accomplish assigned missions; it does not, in and of itself, include authoritative direction for logistics or matters of administration, discipline, internal organization, or unit training.

Tactical Control (TACON): Command authority over assigned or attached forces or commands, or military capability or forces made available for tasking that is limited to the detailed direction and control of movements or maneuvers within the operational area necessary to accomplish missions or tasks assigned. Tactical control is inherent in operational control. Tactical control may be delegated to, and exercised at any level at or below the level of combatant command. When forces are transferred between combatant commands, the command relationship the gaining commander will exercise (and the losing commander will relinquish) over these forces must be specified by the Secretary of Defense. Tactical control provides sufficient authority for controlling and directing the application of force or tactical use of combat support assets within the assigned mission or task.

Bibliography

Advisory Panel to Assess Domestic Response Capabilities for Terrorism Involving Weapons of Mass Destruction, Second Annual Report, *Toward a National Strategy for Combating Terrorism*, December 15, 2000, known as the second Gilmore Commission Report.

_____, Fourth Annual Report, *Implementing the National Strategy*, December 15, 2002, known as the fourth Gilmore Commission Report.

Baca, Lieutenant General Edward D., "Reserve Component Budget Oversight: Statement Before the Subcommittee on Defense, Committee on Appropriations, U.S. Senate, 1st Session, 104th Congress, FY96," May 9, 1995.

Blum, Lieutenant General H. Steven, Chief of the National Guard Bureau, remarks to the National Governors Association meeting, February 22, 2004.

_____, Chief of the National Guard Bureau, discussion with Richard Brennan, June 19, 2003, McLean, Va.

Bremer, L. Paul, III, and Edwin Meese III, A Report of The Heritage Foundation Homeland Security Task Force, *Defending the American Homeland*, January 2002.

Brennan, Richard R., *Protecting the Homeland: Insights from Army Wargames*, Santa Monica, Calif.: RAND Corporation, MR-1490-A, 2002.

Brown, Roger Allen, William Fedorochko, Jr., and John F. Schank, *Assessing the State and Federal Missions of the National Guard*, Santa Monica, Calif.: RAND Corporation, MR-557-OSD, 1995.

Burns, Major General Julian, "Army Support for Homeland Security," briefing for the Association of the United States Army, Washington, D.C.: Department of the Army, July 7, 2003.

Chu, David S. C., Under Secretary of Defense (Personnel and Resources), "Addendum to Mobilization/Demobilization Personnel and Pay Policy for Reserve Component Members Ordered to Active Duty in Response to the World Trade Center and Pentagon Attacks," memorandum, July 19, 2002.

Cody, Lieutenant General Richard A., Deputy Chief of Staff, G-3, and Lieutenant General Franklin L. Hagenbeck, Deputy Chief of Staff, G-1, testimony before Committee on Armed Services, Subcommittee on Total Force, U.S. House of Representatives, 108th Congress, 2nd Session, March 10, 2004.

Congressional Budget Office (CBO), *An Analysis of the U.S. Military's Ability to Sustain an Occupation of Iraq*, Washington, D.C.: Congressional Research Service, 2003.

_____, *Structuring the Active and Reserve Army for the 21st Century*, Washington, D.C.: Congressional Budget Office, 1997.

Congressional Research Service (CRS), *Homeland Security and the Reserves: Threat, Mission, and Force Structure Issues*, Washington, D.C.: CRS, 2002.

Davis, Lynn E., and Jeremy Shapiro, eds., *The U.S. Army and the New National Security Strategy*, Santa Monica, Calif.: RAND Corporation, MR-1657-A, 2003.

Davis, Paul K., James H. Bigelow, and Jimmie McEver, *Analytical Methods for Studies and Experiments on "Transforming the Force,"* Santa Monica, Calif.: RAND Corporation, DB-278-OSD, 1999.

Delk, James D., *Fire and Furies: The L.A. Riots,* Palm Springs, Calif.: ETC Publications, 1995.

Demaine, Linda J., and Brian Rosen, *Reconsidering and Redressing the Posse Comitatus Act,* Santa Monica, Calif.: RAND Corporation, MG-119, forthcoming.

Department of Defense (DoD), *Department of Defense Plan for Integrating National Guard and Reserve Component Support for Response to Attacks Using Weapons of Mass Destruction*, Washington, D.C., January 1998.

_____, *Defense Manpower Requirements Report Fiscal Year 2000*, Washington, D.C.: Office of the Under Secretary of Defense for Personnel and Readiness, June 1999.

_____, *Dictionary of Military Terms*, Joint Publication 1-02, as amended through June 5, 2003b.

_____, DoDD 3025.1, Military Support to Civil Authorities (MSCA), January 15, 1993.

_____, DoDD 3025.12, The DoD Civil Disturbance Plan (Garden Plot), 1994.

_____, DoDD 3025.15, Military Assistance to Civil Authorities (MACA), February 18, 1997.

_____, DoDD 5525.5, *DoD Cooperation with Civilian Law Enforcement Officials,* 1986.

_____, "The DoD Role in Homeland Security," *Defense Study and Report to Congress*, Washington, D.C., July 2003c.

_____, "National Guard Bureau Chief Briefing on the Transforming Roles of the National Guard," news transcript, Washington, D.C., May 16, 2003a, available at http://www.defenselink.mil/transcripts/2003/tr20030516-0188.html.

_____, *Report to Congress on the Role of the Department of Defense in Supporting Homeland Security*, Washington, D.C., September 2003d.

_____, *Homeland Security Joint Operating Concept*, February 2004.

_____, Office of the Assistant Secretary of Defense for Reserve Affairs, Review of Reserve Component Contributions to National Defense, Washington, D.C.: Department of Defense, December 20, 2002.

Department of the Army, *Fiscal Year (FY) 2004/FY 2005 Biennial Budget Estimates, Operation and Maintenance, Army National Guard,* Washington, D.C., February 2003.

_____, *How the Army Runs: A Senior Leader Reference Handbook 2001– 2002*, Carlisle, Pa.: U.S. Army War College, 2001, at http://www.carlisle.army.mil/usawc/dclm/linkedtextchapters.htm.

Dewar, James A., Carl H. Builder, William M. Hix, and Morlie H. Levin, *Assumption-Based Planning: A Planning Tool for Very Uncertain Times*, Santa Monica, Calif.: RAND Corporation, MR-114-A, 1993.

Dillion, Col. Dick, James Kievit, and Lt. Col. Thomas Murray, "Portraying the Army Reserve Components in Army War Games and Exercises," Carlisle, Pa.: Army War College, Center for Strategic Leadership, November 2002.

Eres, Major General Thomas W., Chief, Homeland Security, State of California, "Homeland Security Enhancement Act: Concept Plan Overview," slide presentation at the RAND Corporation, Arlington, Va., June 19, 2002.

Feiler, Jeremy, "National Guard Association: Governors Should Control Deployments," *Inside the Pentagon*, October 10, 2002, p. 1.

5th Signal Command, *Efficient Basing–East Briefing*, undated.

Fleming, Col. Michael P., "National Security Roles for the National Guard," *Journal of Homeland Security*, August 2001, available at http://www.homelandsecurity.org/journal/Articles/Fleming.htm.

General Accounting Office (GAO), *Homeland Defense: Preliminary Observations on How Overseas and Domestic Missions Impact DoD Forces*, statement of Raymond J. Decker, Director Defense Capabilities and Management, Washington, D.C.: GAO, GAO-03-677T, April 29, 2003.

Hall, Thomas F., Assistant Secretary of Defense for Reserve Affairs, Media Roundtable, November 19, 2002.

Helmly, James R., Lieutenant General, Chief Army Reserve, presentation to Reserve Officers Association Meeting, January 27, 2004.

Heritage Foundation, *Defending the American Homeland: A Report of The Heritage Foundation Homeland Security Task Force*, Washington, D.C.: Heritage Foundation, 2002.

Hess, Pamela, "Army Reserve Chief Plans Major Changes," *Washington Times*, January 20, 2004.

Kellman, Barry, *Managing Terrorism's Consequences: Legal Issues,* Washington, D.C.: Memorial Institute for the Prevention of Terrorism, March 2002.

Kent, Glenn A., and David A. Ochmanek, *A Framework for Modernization Within the United States Air Force,* Santa Monica, Calif.: RAND Corporation, MR-1706-AF, 2003.

Krause, Mickie, Fred Dolan, Birger Bergesen II, and Alan Summy, *Homeland Security: Defining the Needs and Missions Amid the Frenzy*, McLean, Va.: Science Applications International Corporation, August 15, 2002.

Krepinevich, Andrew, "Whither the Army," Center for Strategic and Budgetary Assessments, Washington, D.C., 2000, available at http://www.csbaonline.org/4Publications/Archive/H.20000118.Whither_the_Army/H.20000118.Whither_the_Army.htm, accessed August 5, 2004.

Larson, Eric V., and John E. Peters, *Preparing the U.S. Army for Homeland Security: Concepts, Issues, and Options,* Santa Monica, Calif.: RAND Corporation, MR-1251-A, 2001.

Los Angeles Board of Police Commissioners, *The City in Crisis: A Report on the Civil Disorder in Los Angeles*, October 21, 1992.

McDonnell, Janet, *Hurricane Andrew Historical Report,* Fort Belvoir, Va.: Office of History, U.S. Army Corps of Engineers, 1993.

Monroe, Major General Paul D., Jr., The Adjutant General, California National Guard, *Homeland Security Strategy*, Sacramento, Calif.: California Military Department, December 20, 2002.

National Academy of Public Administration, *The Role of the National Guard in Emergency Preparedness and Response*, Washington, D.C., January 1997.

National Guard Association of the United States and the Adjutants General Association of the United States, "Point Paper on Homeland Security," Washington, D.C., February 2002, available at http://www.ngaus.org.

National Guard Bureau, "Report to Congress: Enhancing the National Guard's Readiness to Support Emergency Responders in Domestic Chemical and Biological Terrorism Defense," Washington, D.C., July 20, 1999.

_____, "State Force Structure Recap," spreadsheet, Washington, D.C., undated.

Office of Homeland Security, Office of the President, *The National Security Strategy for Homeland Security*, Washington, D.C., July 2002.

Office of the Secretary of Defense (OSD), *The Annual Report of the Reserve Forces Policy Board: Data Based on Fiscal Year 2000*, Washington, D.C.: Office of the Secretary of Defense, 2001.

Owens, Dallas D., Jr., "AC/RC Integration: Today's Success and Transformation's Challenge," Carlisle, Pa.: Strategic Studies Institute, U.S. Army War College, 2001.

Pirnie, Bruce R., and Corazon M. Francisco, *Assessing Requirements for Peacekeeping, Humanitarian Assistance, and Disaster Relief*, Santa Monica, Calif.: RAND Corporation, MR-951-OSD, 1998.

RAND Arroyo Center, *Annual Report 2001*, Santa Monica, Calif.: RAND Corporation, SB-7062-A, 2002.

Roosevelt, Ann, "Army Reorganization Aims for 2007 Completion," *Defense Daily*, February 19, 2004.

Sarcione, Colonel Stephen, "National Guard Bureau Full-Time Support Division," slide presentation to the AGR Manager's Technical Assistance Workshop, Washington, D.C.: National Guard Bureau, January 22, 2003.

Schnaubelt, Christopher M., "Lessons in Command and Control from the Los Angeles Riots," *Parameters*, Summer 1997, pp. 88–109.

Sortor, Ronald E., *Army Active/Reserve Mix: Force Planning for Major Regional Contingencies*, Santa Monica, Calif.: RAND Corporation, MR-545A, 1995.

Stilley, Colonel Kenneth J., California Army National Guard, interview by authors, June 18, 2003.

Thaler, David E., *Strategies to Tasks: A Framework for Linking Means and Ends*, Santa Monica, Calif.: RAND Corporation, MR-300-AF, 1993.

Thie, Harry J., Ray Conley, Henry Leonard, Megan Abbott, Eric Larson, Scott McMahon, Michael G. Shanley, Ron Sortor, William Taylor, Stephen Dalzell, and Roland Yardley, *Past and Future: Insights for Reserve Component Use*, Santa Monica, Calif.: RAND Corporation, DRR-3022-OSD, August 2003.

U.S. Army, U.S. Army Forces Command, "Briefings for FORSCOM SFOR 6 Planning Update Conference," February 23, 1999.

U.S. Army National Guard, "Force Structure," available at http://www.arng.army.mil/about_us/organization/force_structure.asp.

U.S. Army Research, Development, and Engineering Command (USARDEC), *News Release*, September 29, 2003, available at http://www.rdecom.army.mil/pressrelease29Sep.pdf.

U.S. Commission on National Security/21st Century, *Road Map for National Security: Imperative for Change*, Phase III Report, March 15, 2001, known as the Hart-Rudman Commission.

White House, The, Budget for Fiscal Year 2004, Washington, D.C., 2003.

Winthrop, Jim, "The Oklahoma City Bombing: Immediate Response Authority and Other Military Assistance to Civil Authority (MACA)," *The Army Lawyer,* July 1997, pp. 3, 9–11.